Auschwitz Testimonies

Auschwitz Testimonies
1945–1986

Primo Levi
with Leonardo De Benedetti
Edited by Fabio Levi and Domenico Scarpa
Introduction by Robert S. C. Gordon
Translated by Judith Woolf

polity

First published in Italian as *Così fu Auschwitz. Testimonianze 1945–1986*
© Giulio Einaudi editore s.p.a., Turin, 2015

The translation of this work has been funded by SEPS
SEGRETARIATO EUROPEO PER LE PUBBLICAZIONI SCIENTIFICHE

Via Val d'Aposa 7 – 40123 Bologna – Italy
seps@seps.it – www.seps.it

Chapter 1, Report on the Sanitary and Medical Organization of the Monowitz
Concentration Camp for Jews, first published in English in *Auschwitz Report* (Verso,
2006). Reprinted with permission from Verso Books.

English translation of Chapter 1 © Judith Woolf, 2006

This English edition (excluding Chapter 1) © Polity Press, 2018

Polity Press
65 Bridge Street
Cambridge CB2 1UR, UK

Polity Press
101 Station Landing
Suite 300,
Medford, MA 02155
USA

ISBN-13: 978-1-5095-1336-9
ISBN-13: 978-1-5095-1337-6 (paperback)

A catalogue record for this book is available from the British Library.

Library of Congress Cataloging-in-Publication Data

Names: Levi, Primo, author. | Benedetti, Leonardo De, author.
Title: Auschwitz testimonies, 1945–1986 / Primo Levi, Leonardo De Benedetti.
Other titles: Rapporto sulla organizzazione igienico-sanitaria del campo di
    concentramento per Ebrei di Monowitz (Auschwitz – Alta Slesia). English
Description: Cambridge, UK : Polity Press, [2017] | Includes bibliographical references.
Identifiers: LCCN 2017010122 (print) | LCCN 2017010642 (ebook) |
    ISBN 9781509513369 (hardback) | ISBN 9781509513376 (pbk.) |
    ISBN 9781509513390 (Mobi) | ISBN 9781509513406 (Epub)
Subjects: LCSH: Auschwitz (Concentration camp)–Sanitation. | Monowitz
    (Concentration camp)–Medical Services. | Concentration camp inmates–Health and
    hygiene–Poland–Oświęcim.
Classification: LCC D805.5.A96 L4713 2017 (print) | LCC D805.5.A96 (ebook) | DDC
    940.53/1853862–dc23
LC record available at https://lccn.loc.gov/2017010122

Typeset in 10.5 on 12 pt Sabon Roman
by Toppan Best-set Premedia Limited
Printed and bound in the UK by CPI Group Ltd, Croydon, CR0 4YY

The publisher has used its best endeavours to ensure that the URLs for external websites
referred to in this book are correct and active at the time of going to press. However, the
publisher has no responsibility for the websites and can make no guarantee that a site
will remain live or that the content is or will remain appropriate.

Every effort has been made to trace all copyright holders, but if any have been
inadvertently overlooked the publisher will be pleased to include any necessary credits in
any subsequent reprint or edition.

For further information on Polity, visit our website:
politybooks.com

Contents

Figures

Translator's Note

Judith Woolf

Given the status of many of these documents as an unmediated part of the historical record, I have followed the criteria already adopted by Fabio Levi and Domenico Scarpa in the Italian text by preserving irregularities of spelling and errors in the dating of events or in recalling the number or the names of fellow prisoners. On the basis of the same criteria, I have not standardized the various forms in which the German word *Lager* (camp) appears. I have translated the Italian word *crematorio* as 'crematory' rather than 'crematorium', to make the distinction between a mass incineration plant and a civilized funeral facility. Documents recorded and transcribed by Colonel Massimo Adolfo Vitale, the founder of the Comitato Ricerche Deportati Ebrei (Search Committee for Jewish Deportees), bear the unmistakable signs of his indignation in the capitalizing of key words and the addition of multiple exclamation marks to the otherwise sober prose in which both Primo Levi and Leonardo De Benedetti offer their testimony.

The first document in the book, the 'Report on the Sanitary and Medical Organization of the Monowitz Concentration Camp for Jews', was originally published in Italy in a medical journal whose readers would have known, for instance, that famine oedema is a form of dropsy caused by malnutrition; that phlegmons are inflammations of the subcutaneous connective tissue, leading to ulceration and the formation of invasive abscesses; and that Panflavin, grotesquely employed to treat diphtheria in the camp infirmary, was a brand of throat lozenge. Such details matter because they reveal the stark facts of a time and place in which human beings were condemned to die from diarrhoea and diphtheria and invasive ulcers as deliberately as they were condemned to die by gas. For a complete glossary of the medical and pharmaceutical terms used in the 'Report', see Primo Levi and Leonardo De Benedetti, *Auschwitz Report*, trans. Judith Woolf, ed. Robert S. C. Gordon (London: Verso, 2006), pp. 79–88.

Introduction: Bare Witness

Robert S. C. Gordon

Primo Levi's work has become something of a touchstone of Holocaust writing and of the moral authority of the survivor to give voice to the very worst sufferings of the twentieth century. In 1944–5, Levi spent almost a year battling against the humiliations and deprivations of a prisoner's half-life in Auschwitz – specifically Auschwitz-III, the concentration and labour camp near Monowitz [Monowice] – and nearly another year, following his miraculous survival and liberation, on a tortuous, stop–start journey home from Poland to Turin. His writings first emerged, locally, almost invisibly, in Turin in 1947, starting with the small-scale publication of *If This is a Man*, a pellucid exploration of the human body and the human mind as it adapted to life, or rather non-life, at Auschwitz. His profile and authority grew a little in the 1950s and 1960s, including glimmerings of an international presence, following the republication of that first book and the appearance of its sister volume, *The Truce* (1963), the story of his meandering return across the wastelands of post-war central Europe. He continued to write, publish, speak, and all the while work at his daytime profession as an industrial chemist. In a quite unique and unclassifiable book, *The Periodic Table* (1975), he brought to the page a fizzing chronicle of his life in/through chemistry, overshadowed only occasionally by memories of Fascism, anti-Semitism and genocide. The

1980s brought a step-change in his international reputation, with bestselling translations and lionization in the English-speaking world, crowned by the publication of his final book of essays on the Holocaust and its moral and historical legacy forty years on, *The Drowned and the Saved* (1986). His death in 1987, almost certainly by suicide, prompted genuine and widespread grief at the loss of such a voice, such a companion in dialogue, such testimony.[1]

Levi himself was one of the first and most eloquent writers to embrace the terminology of testimony. It is there, for example, in one of the most powerful passages of *If This is a Man* (of the 1958 second edition, that is: the passage is not in the 1947 edition):[2] in the very early days after Levi's arrival in Auschwitz, Steinlauf, a former officer of the Austro-Hungarian army and now a filthy shell of a man mired in Auschwitz, teaches Levi his first lesson in the persistence of human dignity:

> It grieves me now that I have forgotten his plain, clear words, the words of ex-Sergeant Steinlauf of the Austro-Hungarian Army, Iron Cross in the 1914–1918 war. It grieves me because it means that I have to translate his uncertain Italian and his quiet speech, the speech of a good soldier, into my language of an incredulous man. But this was the sense, not forgotten then or later: that precisely because the Lager was a great machine to reduce us to beasts, we must not become beasts; that even in this place one can survive, and therefore one must want to survive, to tell the story, to bear witness.
>
> (*The Complete Works of Primo Levi*, p. 37)

---

[1] Levi's remarkable reputation in the English-speaking world has continued to grow in the three decades since his death, sealed by the recent publication of a major, complete, re-edited and re-translated edition of his oeuvre in English, a unique accolade for an Italian writer: see *The Complete Works of Primo Levi*, ed. Ann Goldstein, 3 vols. (New York: Liveright, 2015).

[2] The latest edition of Levi's works in Italian includes full versions of both the standard 1958 edition of *If This is a Man* and the previously untraceable 1947 edition (*Opere complete di Primo Levi*, ed. Marco Belpoliti, 2 vols. (Turin: Einaudi, 2016), pp. 3–133 (1947 edition), pp. 135–277 (1958 edition)).

That other great Holocaust survivor-writer Elie Wiesel, perhaps the only one who is Levi's equal in terms of the moral force and clarity of their work, eloquently captured the specific power of this vocation for testimony, as a vessel for containing in words the scale and the inhuman extremes of the Shoah: 'if the Greeks invented tragedy, the Romans the epistle and the Renaissance the sonnet, our generation invented a new literature, that of testimony'.[3] As Wiesel's formulation suggests, this new literature of 'testimony' – the writing of and out of suffering, from the bare body of the victim at the edge of death, to the essentially human act of voicing, of stating that 'this happened' (as Levi's poem at the start of *If This is a Man* baldly puts it) – has hidden depths. It has the force, complexity and depth of literature, of the profoundest forms of expression that the civilization of the word has invented, even if the terminology of testimony suggests the legalistically mute courtroom witness (one who must neither comment nor elaborate, who is a camera lens, a microphone, a vessel more than a voice). Levi's published work taken as a whole – much like Wiesel's, although in profoundly different ways – shows him constantly striving to go beyond bare witnessing, inventing multiple, complex dynamics for testimony, rich hybrids of neutral record and literary elaboration, in a searching, attentive, balanced style that is yet acutely attuned to fracture, hesitation and muted confusion. Levi's testimony is a fluid, sophisticated layering of truths, from fact to reflection, from court deposition to writerly composition.

There are risks as well as rewards in navigating this path, however, since it is also a path between fact and the tools of fiction. In recent critical debate on Levi's work, there has been a fascinating discussion of one telling case in point, the chapter of *The Periodic Table* called 'Vanadium', in which Levi recounts his chance contact in the 1960s with one of the German chemists who had briefly been his supervisor in the factory laboratory where Levi had been assigned as a slave labourer for a few weeks at Monowitz. This German, called

[3] Elie Wiesel, 'The Holocaust as Literary Inspiration', in *Dimensions of the Holocaust* (Evanston, Ill.: Northwestern University Press, 1977), pp. 4–19 (p. 19).

Müller in the story, had on occasion acted kindly towards him in the camp; but he was a German, on the other side, part of the system of persecution at Auschwitz, part of the Nazi state, a bystander actively complicit with genocide. He was, in other words, deep within what Levi would later call 'the grey zone'. In 'Vanadium', Levi and Müller correspond; Levi is hesitant, unsure, unwilling to offer the impossible absolution that Müller seems to want from him, and troubled by the unsettling effect that this encounter has had on him. Before they can meet, Müller dies, suddenly, a difficult dialogue is cut short, perhaps necessarily. Biographers and critics have since discovered that 'Vanadium' is a remarkable mix of fact and narrative reshaping: Müller's real name was Ferdinand Meyer, and Levi had asked a friend and intermediary to trace him, and several other figures he remembered from the camps, rather than stumbling across him by chance, spotting a misspelled word that triggers a flash of memory; and the two had spoken and possibly even met before Meyer's death. In other words, Levi reshaped the episode seven years on for *The Periodic Table*, in an effort to express adequately the tense legacies and complex truths of complicity and individual humanity in the 'grey' figure of the bystander.[4]

Testimony, then, at least in the hands of a writer of Levi's subtlety, is best thought of as malleable and fluid in form, and as one all the more profoundly engaged with truths historical, moral and imaginative for that. If it is practised and applied too narrowly, it risks becoming a straitjacket, as if the survivor were being told not to try out new ways of seeing, new ways of voicing, to stick to what s/he saw and heard, courtroom-style. In this sense, Levi's essays, his newspaper columns, his poems, his anthologies, his translations, his science-fiction and fantasy, his novels and stories of work, resistance and science – his entire eclectic body of work, whatever its many other virtues and qualities, can be said

---

[4] For 'Vanadium', see Levi's biographers Carole Angier, *The Double Bond. Primo Levi: A Biography* (London: Viking, Penguin, 2002), pp. 579–83; Ian Thomson's *Primo Levi* (London: Hutchinson, 2002), pp. 305–10, 250–2; and Marco Belpoliti, 'Vanadio e il grigio dottor Müller', in *Primo Levi di fronte e di profilo* (Parma: Guanda, 2015), pp. 261–73; Martina Mengoni, *Primo Levi e i tedeschi / Primo Levi and the Germans* (Turin: Einaudi, 2017).

also to express this mode of flexible testimony: the on-going elaboration of a reflection on the fact that 'this happened'. Perhaps more than any other survivor-writer, Levi's practice of testimony was capacious, stretching the definition and the boundaries of Wiesel's grim twentieth-century invention.

Which brings us to this remarkable collection of fragments, *Auschwitz Testimonies: 1945–1986*, painstakingly compiled and edited by Fabio Levi and Domenico Scarpa of the Centro Primo Levi in Turin. *Auschwitz Testimonies* is not a new book by Primo Levi as such, certainly not one of those often unsatisfactory posthumous fragments of an incomplete work.[5] Nor is it a mere miscellany of occasional articles, however.[6] This is because it has a powerful coherence as a collection and the editors have a powerful point to make with it: that beneath the surface of Levi's extraordinary creative testimony carried out across his published oeuvre – his lifelong work of observation, truth-telling and reflective, imaginative elaboration – there lies another layer of testimony, a hidden seam in the work of witness, sustained just like the layer above it across the four long decades of Levi's post-war career, indeed integral to it.

Auschwitz Testimonies contains around two dozen short documents by Primo Levi, accompanied by a handful written by or with his older friend and fellow Auschwitz survivor, Leonardo De Benedetti, all fragments of the most direct, raw attempts at setting the record or setting it straight. These documents – some familiar, others entirely new, unpublished or long forgotten, recovered by the editors from obscure archives, journals and catalogues – are in many respects typical of the detritus of words left behind by the past, only

[5] Readers of Levi's biographies will know that there exists an incomplete manuscript of a final work by Levi, provisionally entitled 'The Double Bond' ('Il doppio legame'), conceived as a companion volume to *The Periodic Table*. To date, there is no sign that this unfinished work will be published (Angier, *Double Bond*, pp. 672–86; Thomson, *Primo Levi*, pp. 351–7).

[6] See, e.g., Primo Levi, *The Black Hole of Auschwitz* (Cambridge: Polity, 2003), a selection of those 'Occasional Writings', including versions of four of the short pieces included in *Auschwitz Testimonies*, although with certain variations. A near-exhaustive section of uncollected writings is included in *The Complete Works of Primo Levi*.

a fraction of which are destined to survive, ready for rediscovery by diligent future historians. There is a professional technical report, an exchange of letters, signed statements and legal questionnaires, lists, notes, brief occasional articles. This is Levi (and De Benedetti) busy at a low-level, behind-the-scenes, quiet and sporadic labour: a sort of minimal or bare witnessing, all but unelaborated, in contrast to the complex elaborations of the published work, but neither reductive nor restrictive for that.

Many of the pieces are partial, provisional, often marked by uncertainty and even error – a good example is the distorted figure, originating in Soviet documents that circulated for many years after the war, of 4 million victims at Auschwitz, which is used here by Levi (e.g. in 'This Was Auschwitz'; or 5 million in 'Political Deportees'; 3.5 million in 'That Train to Auschwitz'). Later research has corrected this number to only (only!) just over 1 million, of the 6 million Jewish victims of genocide all told. Even in their personal recollections, Levi and De Benedetti contradict themselves and each other on minor details, such as over the exact number on their deportation trucks or the ages of the oldest and youngest victims on the convoy. Were a historian to come upon these fragments in their research, they would no doubt look for corroboration and correction from dozens of other sources; perhaps, were their author's name not one so well known and admired, they would be set to one side, to disappear once more into the vast war archive. But we do not need to read these traces of the past and of the work of testimony they enact quite like professional historians. There are other truths, other kinds of human and humanizing effort at stake here.

The book's mosaic of documents reflects different moments in Levi's career as a public and private witness, as a researcher and writer, and the form they take reflects the different kinds of requests and contexts that produced them. Several are interestingly strained or constrained by their form (and the slips and gaps are one symptom of this): we should not go looking for the powerful rhetoric and equipoise of Levi's books here. On the contrary, the strain is a marker of the distinctive value these pieces hold: their struggle to get clear facts and essential truths down on paper, unadorned, their quiet work of transmission.

We can identify five loose types of document in these *Auschwitz Testimonies*. The first and longest entry in the book also gives us possibly the most surprising type of the five: this is a 1946 medical and hygienic report on the sanitary conditions at Monowitz, a document that Levi drafted together with De Benedetti – in all probability, in fact, De Benedetti took the lead here, as he was a professional physician – while they were both in a Soviet holding camp at Kattowitz [Katowice], following liberation from Auschwitz in early 1945.[7] The Soviets asked many Auschwitz survivors, and especially doctors, to set down on record their observations as they prepared their own state report on Nazi atrocities. On their return home to Turin, De Benedetti and Levi refined it and submitted it to a local professional medical journal, *Minerva Medica*, where it was published in late 1946 with all its dry detail of pathologies, nutrition, patent medications and treatments in the camp, in particular in its awful clinic (later the subject of a potent chapter in *If This is a Man*, 'Ka Be'), in reality more likely an entry-point to the gas chambers than a place of care or cure.

Like the medical report, the second type of bare witnessing sampled here also has its origins in the ferment of the weeks and months immediately following Levi's return. Writing, talking, thinking and pushing in many directions as he struggled to come to terms with what he had experienced, Levi was variously drafting chapters of *If This is a Man*, writing poems, strange fictions, war tales and Auschwitz memories, as well as starting a career, meeting his future wife, working on the medical report with De Benedetti, and looking to help discover who of his many companions survived and who did not, amongst all those whose paths he had crossed since he had taken refuge in the Alps in late 1943. A cluster of documents in *Auschwitz Testimonies* – the briefest but also in some ways the most talismanic and moving of them all – sees Levi leaving traces of these people in the archive.

---

[7] The report was rediscovered by critic Alberto Cavaglion and published in Italian in 1993, and a first English edition appeared as *Auschwitz Report* (London: Verso, 2006). The version published here has been revised following the corrected edition first published in Italian in 2013.

Especially pregnant are the bare lists, one present here also in facsimile image, where Levi transcribes and recovers as many names as he can from the maelstrom. From 1945, there is a report listing the names he can recall of those evacuated from Monowitz on the Nazi death marches as the Soviets closed in; from 1971, there is another list, of seventy-six names: those who were with him on his first entry into Monowitz. (The several hundred others who had reached Auschwitz on the same train as Levi and De Benedetti were, of course, gassed immediately on arrival.) Levi annotates his list, with precision and hideous, necessary clarity: letter codes, symbols and boxes stand for different nationalities and categories: those who died of illness, those in selections for the gas chambers, those deported elsewhere, the few (fourteen) who survived.[8]

These lists have a bare power in their own right, but from as early as 1945 and throughout the post-war decades, such information-gathering was also pursued with a specific further purpose in mind: prosecution of Nazi perpetrators. Trial documents are the third and most numerous type on display in *Auschwitz Testimonies*, also the type where De Benedetti stands most consistently and steadily alongside Levi, the two giving evidence for the same trials, on occasion travelling abroad to provide depositions, but more often drafting clipped, short documents in Italy for prosecutors' files. Here, the two are literal witnesses, deposed for the prosecution. In 1946–7, for example, both provide generic statements for Italian-Jewish research authorities on their experience of and conditions in Monowitz, drawing on their medical report and on their lists. They also draft declarations for the trial of Auschwitz camp commandant Rudolf Höss, tried and executed in Poland in 1947. In 1959–60, De Benedetti documents his knowledge of his fellow doctor and infamous torturer Joseph Mengele, as part of failed West German efforts at extradition and prosecution. Around the same time, Levi provides a deposition for the Jerusalem trial of the prime bureaucrat and architect of the Final Solution, Adolf Eichmann. (Levi also writes a powerful article on Eichmann for a cultural journal,

---

[8] Levi refers to the list as an attachment in his 'Deposition for the Bosshammer Trial'. Further lists of names are included in Levi's 'Deposition for the Eichmann Trial' and both Levi's and De Benedetti's 'Questionnaire for the Bosshammer Trial'.

included here as 'Testimony for Eichmann', and a devastating poem, 'For Adolf Eichmann': *The Complete Works of Primo Levi*, p. 1906). Both friends, finally, contribute in the 1960s and again in the early 1970s, to the long process of evidence-gathering leading to the war-crimes prosecution of Friedrich Bosshammer, Eichmann's lieutenant and operator of the Final Solution in Italy. Bosshammer was sentenced to life imprisonment in 1972, for the murder of more than 3,000 Italian Jews, on the basis of research coordinated by West German prosecutors and CDEC, a Milanese Jewish research centre, who gathered Levi and De Benedetti's evidence – declarations, questionnaires and depositions – alongside that of many others. Bosshammer died only a few months later, before the final verdict was confirmed.

The last two forms of bare witnessing sampled here draw on Levi's public occasional writings and press articles (e.g. for the Turin national daily *La Stampa*, for a Jewish community magazine *Ha Keillah*, and for anti-Fascist or campaigning journals). These are perhaps more familiar kinds of writing – these or comparable pieces have been anthologized before in *The Black Hole of Auschwitz* and elsewhere. They belong to the more civic and public role Levi increasingly took on over the last twenty to thirty years of his life, as he became the single most prominent and powerful Holocaust voice in Italy (and in due course internationally also). These strands find a starting-point as far back as 1955, however, in a piece called 'Anniversary', a short article but a watershed in this trajectory from private to public. In it, Levi uses the tenth anniversary of Italy's liberation and the end of the war to lay down several lines of future Holocaust memory, lamenting the silence that surrounds the genocide and calling for renewed, honest attention to all its horrors (honest because Levi writes here, perhaps for the first time, about the shame of the camps, the degradations and complicities they forced on their victims, later one of the great themes of *The Drowned and the Saved*). Further anniversary pieces follow from 1960 and again 1975. The 1960 article (published 1961, 'Deportation and Exportation of the Jews') draws on Levi's contribution to one of several major cycles of public lectures and talks, on Fascism and the war, that took place in Italian cities to mark the fifteenth anniversary of 1945, and coincided with events to commemorate the centenary of Italy's modern nationhood and, indeed, with a recent flowering of neo-Fascism in Italy. (This talk, given in Bologna, was one of the rare occasions when Levi shared a public platform with the other great Italian-Jewish writer and chronicler of Fascist anti-Semitism, Giorgio Bassani.)

From the late 1950s and for the following decades, another crucial strand of civic engagement with Holocaust memorialization opened up for Levi: Holocaust exhibitions and monuments. *Auschwitz Testimonies* gives us three examples of such sites and Levi's contributions and responses: in Turin in 1959, a travelling exhibition on deportation of anti-Fascists, Jews and other victims from Italy to the concentration camps produced a remarkable outpouring of interest, especially among the younger generations, which touched Levi deeply. He calls it here the 'Miracle in Turin' in one article and publishes a fascinating exchange of letters with a young girl who signs herself, 'A Fascist's daughter who wants to know the truth', which allows him to address the confusions of the young and Italy's failure to reflect on its long, generational complicity with Fascism. (The final piece published here, 'To Our Generation...', shows this generational perspective stayed with Levi until the end.) The letters bring out a pedagogical impulse in Levi's voice, one carried through to his contributions to Italian Holocaust museums and memorials. In 1973, he pens a piece ('The Europe of the Lagers') for a new national Museum of Deportation, displaying objects from the camps, letters from victims executed by Nazis, and artworks by Picasso, Léger, Guttuso and others, which opened in the small central-northern town of Carpi, near Bologna. A few miles from Carpi stood Fossoli, the largest detention and pre-deportation camp in Italy, where Levi and De Benedetti were held by Italian Fascists and German SS before transportation to Auschwitz. Fossoli is named in the very first line of the 1947 edition of *If This is a Man* (the 1958 edition added a page on Levi's time as an anti-Fascist partisan prior to his arrest) and is the site of excruciating scenes of premonition:

> Night came, and it was such a night one knew that human eyes would not witness it and survive... All took leave of life in the manner that most suited them. Some prayed, some drank to excess, others became intoxicated by a final unseemly lust. But mothers stayed up to prepare food for the journey with tender

care, and washed their children and packed the luggage; and at dawn the barbed wire was full of children's washing hung out to dry in the wind. Nor did they forget the diapers, the toys, the pillows, and the hundred other small things that mothers remember and children always need. Would you not do the same? If you and your child were going to be killed tomorrow, would you not feed him today?

(*The Complete Works of Primo Levi*, p. 11)

The same collection of artists, survivor groups and civic officials that worked on the Carpi museum also worked on the project for an Italian national memorial and monument at Auschwitz itself, which opened in 1980. Here too, Levi lent his voice, and we can read it in the form of a draft notice here, 'Draft of a Text for the Interior of the Italian Block at Auschwitz': a quite formal (once again, strained) piece of pedagogical writing that synthesizes an arc of history that led from Fascist thugs burning buildings in Italy in 1919–20 to Nazis burning books and then people in 1930s and 1940s Germany and Europe.

Levi's achievements as a writer-witness and as a writer (which are not quite the same thing) would not have been possible without his below-the-radar activity of bare witnessing. But these pieces show us more than just a laboratory source of a great writer's oeuvre (and to have shown this is a signal achievement of Fabio Levi and Domenico Scarpa's work of excavation, editing and commentary). They speak also to a larger enterprise and to something beyond the individual voice. They are minimal moments of a large-scale collective effort at remembering and recording carried out over decades, by individual survivors, families, groups and associations (Levi mentions more than once ANED, an Italian association of ex-deportees to which he dedicated much time and effort), by communities and indeed entire generations. They constantly practise or lean towards forms of contact and transmission, of both facts and awareness, and in this they express a constant facet of Levi, an ethical tension towards others, towards dialogue and attention. For this reason, it is powerfully apt that *Auschwitz Testimonies* is not in fact authored by one single writer, Primo Levi – even one now rightly canonized as a great voice of twentieth-century history and literature. It is rather a shared enterprise, by Primo Levi and Leonardo De Benedetti, fellow victims and fellow witnesses, companions in suffering and indeed friends – as is movingly evident in Primo's commemoration of Leonardo on his death in 1983, 'In Memory of a Good Man', another act of witness; and as had already been powerfully clear as they finally, nervously, together crossed the border back into Italy in Autumn 1945, witnesses to a shared, fragile rebirth:

> After dark we passed the Brenner, which we had crossed into exile twenty months before – our less tested comrades in cheerful tumult, Leonardo and I in a silence charged with memory. Of six hundred and fifty, the number who had left, three of us were returning. And what had we lost, in those twenty months? What should we find at home? How much of ourselves had been eroded, extinguished? Did we return richer or poorer, stronger or weaker? We did not know; but we knew that on the thresholds of our homes, for good or ill, a trial awaited us, and we anticipated it with fear. Flowing through our veins, with the weary blood, we felt the poison of Auschwitz. Where would we draw the strength to resume living, to knock down the barriers, the hedges that grow up on their own during all absences, around every abandoned house, every empty den? Soon, even tomorrow, we would have to join battle, against still unknown enemies, within and outside us. With what weapons, what energy, what will? We felt old with the weight of centuries...
>
> (*The Truce*, in *The Complete Works of Primo Levi*,
> p. 396, adapted)

Характеристика

Леви Примо (из Торино)

За время пребывание при Санитарной
части 125 полевзапури много от-
дал своих сил для блага народа
Своим внимательным чутким от-
ношением к больным, он заслужил
должное внимание от них а так
же от Российского Командование

Благодарим тебя за то что твой
труд очень свят людей во всех
странах мира.

Нач. сан службы 125
капитан [подпись]

Figure 1 Testimonial given to Primo Levi at Kattowitz on 30 June 1945 by the 'Head of Medical Service 125' (Private papers of the Levi family). Levi describes the presentation of the document in *The Truce*, slightly altering its wording: 'Danchenko...took out two testimonials written in a beautiful hand on two sheets of lined paper, evidently torn from an exercise book. My testimonial declared with unconstrained generosity that "Primo Levi, doctor of medicine, of Turin, has given able and assiduous help to the Surgery of this Command for four months, and in this manner has merited the gratitude of all the workers of the world."' (See Primo Levi, *The Truce*, in *If This is a Man and The Truce*, trans. Stuart Woolf (London: Abacus, 1987), p. 282.) The document actually reads as follows:

> Testimonial
> Primo Levi (from Turin)
>
> During his time in Medical Service 125 of the Command he has worked with all his might for the good of the people With his attentive and kindly conduct towards the sick he has deserved due gratitude both from them and from the Russian Command We thank you in order that your work may be appreciated by hundreds of people in all the countries of the world.
>
> The Head of Medical Service 125
> Captain [illegible]
>
> [stamp]
> Petr Vladimirovi Klimcenko
> Doctor

A similar testimonial was given to Leonardo De Benedetti, and is reproduced on p. 38 of Anna Segre's *Un coraggio silenzioso. Leonardo De Benedetti, medico, sopravvissuto ad Auschwitz* [A Silent Courage: Leonardo De Benedetti, Doctor and Auschwitz Survivor] (Turin: Zamorani, 2008).

It was while Levi and De Benedetti were working in the Medical Service at Kattowitz that they were asked by the Soviet authorities to compile the document that later became the *Report on the Sanitary and Medical Organization of the Monowitz Concentration Camp*, which was published in *Minerva Medica* after their return to Italy.

COPIA   1

RAPPORTO SULL'ORGANIZZAZIONE
IGIENICO-SANITARIA DEL CAMPO
DI CONCENTRAMENTO PER EBREI DI
MONOWITZ (AUSHWITZ - ALTA SLESIA)

dott. Leonardo DE-BENEDETTI, medico-chirurgo
dott. Primo LEVI, chimico

        Attraverso i documenti fotografici e le ormai numerose rela-
zioni fornite da ex-internati nei diversi Campi di Concentramento
creati dai tedeschi per l'annientamento degli Ebrei d'Europa, forse
non v'è più alcuno che ignori ancora che cosa siano stati quei luoghi
di sterminio e quali nefandezze vi siano state compiute. Tuttavia,
allo scopo di far meglio conoscere gli orrori di cui anche noi siamo
stati testimoni e spesse volte vittime durante il periodo di un anno,
crediamo utile rendere pubblica in Italia una Relazione che abbiamo
presentata al Governo dell'U.R.S.S., su richiesta del Comando Russo
del Campo di Concentramento di Kattowitz per Italiani ex-prigionieri.
In questo Campo fummo ospitati anche noi, dopo la nostra liberazione
avvenuta da parte dell'Armata Rossa verso la fine del gennaio 1945.
Aggiungiamo qui, a quella relazione, qualche notizia di ordine generale;
poichè il nostro rapporto di allora doveva riguardare esclusivamente
il funzionamento dei Servizi Sanitari del Campo di Monowitz; analoghi
rapporti furono richiesti dallo stesso Governo di Mosca a tutti quei
medici di ogni nazionalità che provenienti da altri campi erano stati
ugualmente liberati.

                                    · · ·

        Eravamo partiti dal Campo di Concentramento di Fossoli di
Carpi (Modena) il 22 febbraio 1944, con un convoglio di 650 ebrei di
ambo i sessi e di ogni età: il più vecchio oltrepassava gli ottant'anni
il più giovane era un lattante di tre mesi. Molti erano ammalati e
alcuni in forma grave; un vecchio settantenne, che era stato colpito
da emorragia cerebrale pochi giorni prima della partenza, fu ugualmente
caricato sul treno e morì durante il viaggio.
        Il treno era composto di soli carri bestiami, chiusi dall'ester
no; in ogni vagone erano state stipate più di cinquanta persone, la
maggior parte delle quali aveva portato con sè quanto più aveva potuto
di valigie, perchè un maresciallo tedesco, addetto al campo di Fossoli
ci aveva suggerito, con l'aria di dare un consiglio spassionato e
affettuoso, di provvederci di molti indumenti pesanti: maglie, coperte,
pellicce, perchè saremmo stati condotti in paesi dal clima più rigido del nostro. E aveva aggiunto, con un sorriso benevolo e una strizzatina d'occhi ironica, che, se qualcuno avesse avuto con sè denari
o gioielli nascosti, avrebbe fatto bene a portare anche quelli, che
lassù gli sarebbero certamente riusciti utili. La maggioranza dei
partenti aveva abboccato, accettando un consiglio che non era altro
che un volgare tranello; altri, pochissimi, avevano preferito affidare

                                                        ./.

Figure 2 Unpublished typescript of first page of the 'Report'
(Istoreto Archive, Turin).

Min. Med

MINERVA MEDICA

TORINO · VIA MARTIRI DELLA LIBERTÀ, 15 (CASELLA POSTALE 491) · TELEF. 82-669

REDAZIONE : E. Anglesio · I. Antonini · R. Bèttica-Giovannini · F. De Matteis · R. De Mattia · A. Ferrari A. Gambigliani-Zoccoli · M. Gianotti · A. Muggia · M. Nizza · D. Origlia · W. Paolino · U. Rondelli · E. Signoris C. Solero · G. Usseglio · U. Vignolo-Lutati · A. Visendaz · E. Zambelli

Corrispondenti : V. C. Alzona (Casale) · G. Barenghi (Genova) · G. Bassi (Bologna) · G. Boccuzzi (Taranto) · L. Gedda (Roma) · G. Giordanengo (Novara) · G. Lenti (Ferrara) · M. Mariotti (Ancona) · F. Pellegrini (Milano) · R. Rossi (Roma) A. Muggia (per il Sud-America) · A. Pedrazzini (per la Svizzera) · S. Rossi (per la Spagna)

Redattore Capo : N. Garosci   Direttore Responsabile : T. Oliaro

Gli abbonamenti decorrono dal 1º Gennaio e si intendono rinnovati se non sono disdetti entro il mese di Dicembre· I manoscritti devono essere dattilografati e non si restituiscono anche se non pubblicati. · I lavori accettati per la stampa sono pubblicati gratuitamente. · Lavori, corrispondenza, assegni, vaglia, vanno indirizzati a " Minerva Medica ,. Casella postale 491 · Via Martiri della Libertà, 15 · Torino.

LA RIVISTA È POSTA SOTTO LA TUTELA DELLE LEGGI INTERNAZIONALI SULLA PROPRIETA' LETTERARIA ABBONAMENTO PER IL 1947 L. 1000 · PER L'ESTERO L. 1600 · IL FASCICOLO L. 80

Anno XXXVII · Vol. II   Conto Corrente Postale n. 2-15808   N. 47 (24 Novembre 1946)

SOMMARIO

Figure 3 Title page of *Minerva Medica*, 24 November 1946.

presenta un evidente ingrossamento, deborda circa tre dita dall'arcata costale sinistra, un po' dura, indolente, liscia. Niente di anormale agli organi urinari e genitali; nulla di patologicamente importante nelle urine. Riflessi superficiali e profondi normali.

In base ai dati anamnestici ed obbiettivi formulai il sospetto di brucellosi e pertanto consigliai di praticare la sierodiagnosi. Essendo questa risultata positiva all'1 : 1000 per la brucellosi, e negativa per il tifo e paratifo, come negativa pure risultò la ricerca del parassita malarico contemporaneamente eseguita, confermai così il sospetto diagnostico, consigliai di iniziare subito la cura col vaccino antimelitense endovenoso dell'I. S. M.

Il giorno 5-5-1946 praticai la prima iniezione endovenosa del suddetto vaccino, continuando in tal modo secondo le regole comuni, fino al giorno 21-5-1946. Secondo la curva termica la paziente ha avuto delle buone reazioni termiche postvacciniche, ma la curva febbrile della malattia restava piuttosto immodificata, come pure il resto della sintomatologia morbosa. Cosicchè, avendo letto proprio in quei giorni del metodo del Prof. D. Campanacci, e non avendo la paziente mostrato nessun miglioramento generale, presentandosi sempre il fegato e la milza aumentati di volume e di consistenza, convinto anche, nel caso speciale, della innocuità del nuovo metodo, sospesi il trattamento vaccinico, di cui avevo già praticato 7 iniezioni a dosi crescenti e praticai due iniezioni endovenose di Neo I.C.I. da centigrammi quindici ciascuna nei giorni 23 e 25 maggio. La curva febbrile rimase immodificata. Il giorno 27 praticai nuovamente il vaccino endovenoso e dall'indomani già si vide un netto miglioramento del fegato e della milza aumentati di volume e di consistenza, anche nel caso speciale, della innocuità del nuovo metodo, sospesi il trattamento vaccinico, di cui avevo già praticato 7 iniezioni a dosi crescenti e praticai abbassamento evidente della temperatura febbrile che raggiunse il massimo di 37°,8. Alla successiva iniezione del 30 maggio il miglioramento fu evidentissimo e si ebbe sfebbramento completo: il 4 giugno praticai l'ultima iniezione di vaccino, a scopo di consolidamento.

Ho visto recentemente la paziente completamente guarita, il cui fegato e la milza sono ritornati al volume normale fin da quando la lasciai.

Questi sono i fatti che dimostrano il risultato veramente brillante ottenuto da questa associazione di medicamenti.

Allo stato attuale degli studi non ci sarebbe che emettere soltanto delle ipotesi sul meccanismo di azione dell'associazione vaccino-arsenobenzoli; sarei del parere anch'io che gli arsenobenzoli a dosi piccole, come in questo caso, esercitino una influenza sul fegato e sugli organi emo-linfopoietici in genere, stimolando beneficamente tutti i organi, sedi principali del processo brucellare, a reagire in modo più energico contro i germi dell'infezione in atto, rendendoli più sensibili a nuova introduzione di vaccino.

A mio modo di vedere il metodo del Prof. D. Campanacci merita di essere esperimentato su larga scala, e spero che altri sanitari lo possano trovare utile come è capitato a me, e se i dati suesposti saranno confermati, sarebbe veramente necessario cercare di spiegare in maniera scientifica, e non soltanto ipotetica, l'intimo meccanismo di azione di tale associazione.

Riassunto. — L'Autore descrive un caso di brucellosi vaccino-resistente sensibilizzata con microdosi di arsenobenzolo endovenoso, secondo il metodo del Prof. Campanacci, ottenendo ottimo risultato.

Propone che siano estesi gli studi sul meccanismo d'azione della associazione vaccino-arsenobenzolo.

Rapporto sulla organizzazione igienico-sanitaria del campo di concentramento per Ebrei di Monowitz (Auschwitz - Alta Slesia)

Dott. Leonardo De-Benedetti, *medico-chirurgo*

Dott. Primo Levi, *chimico*

Attraverso i documenti fotografici e le oramai numerose relazioni fornite da ex-internati nei diversi Campi di concentramento creati dai tedeschi per l'annientamento degli Ebrei d'Europa, forse non v'è più alcuno che ignori ancora che cosa siano stati quei luoghi di sterminio e quali nefandezze vi siano state compiute. Tuttavia, allo scopo di far meglio conoscere gli orrori, di cui anche noi siamo stati testimoni e spesse volte vittime durante il periodo di un anno, crediamo utile rendere pubblica in Italia una relazione, che abbiamo presentata al Governo dell'U.R.S.S., su richiesta del Comando Russo del Campo di concentramento di Kattowitz per Italiani ex-prigionieri. In questo Campo fummo ospitati anche noi, dopo la nostra liberazione, avvenuta da parte dell'Armata Rossa verso la fine del gennaio 1945. Aggiungiamo qui, a quella relazione, qualche notizia di ordine generale, poichè il nostro rapporto di allora doveva riguardare esclusivamente il funzionamento dei servizi sanitari del Campo di Monowitz. Analoghi rapporti furono richiesti dallo stesso Governo di Mosca a tutti quei Medici di ogni nazionalità, che, provenienti da altri Campi, erano stati ugualmente liberati.

* * *

Eravamo partiti dal campo di concentramento di Fossoli di Carpi (Modena) il 22 febbraio 1944, con un convoglio di 650 Ebrei di ambo i sessi e di ogni età. Il più vecchio oltrepassava gli 80 anni, il più giovane era un lattante di tre mesi. Molti erano ammalati, e alcuni in forme gravi: un vecchio settantenne, che era stato colpito da emorragia cerebrale pochi giorni prima della partenza, fu ugualmente caricato sul treno e morì durante il viaggio.

Il treno era composto di soli carri bestiame, chiusi dall'esterno; in ogni vagone erano state stipate più di cinquanta persone, la maggior parte delle quali aveva portato con sè quanto più aveva potuto di valigie, perchè un maresciallo tedesco, addetto al Campo di Fossoli, ci aveva suggerito, con l'aria di dare un consiglio spassionato e affettuoso, di provvederci di molti indumenti pesanti — maglie, coperte, pelliccie — perchè saremmo stati condotti in paesi dal clima più rigido del nostro. E aveva aggiunto, con un sorrisetto benevolo e una strizzatina d'occhi ironica, che, se qualcuno avesse avuto con sè denari o gioielli nascosti, avrebbe fatto bene a portare anche quelli, che lassù gli sarebbero certo riusciti utili. La maggioranza dei partenti aveva abboccato, seguendo un consiglio che nascondeva un volgare tranello; altri, pochissimi, avevano preferito affidare a qualche privato che aveva libero accesso nel Campo, le loro robe; altri, infine, che all'atto dell'arresto non avevano avuto il tempo di provve-

1

Report on the Sanitary and Medical Organization of the Monowitz Concentration Camp for Jews (Auschwitz – Upper Silesia)

Dr Leonardo De Benedetti,
physician and surgeon

Dr Primo Levi, chemist

[1945–1946]

The photographic evidence, and the already numerous accounts provided by ex-internees of the various Concentration Camps created by the Germans for the annihilation of the European Jews, mean that there is perhaps no longer anyone still unaware of the nature of those places of extermination and of the iniquities that were committed there. Nevertheless, in order to make better known the horrors of which we too were witnesses and very often victims throughout the course of a year, we believe that it will be useful to make public in Italy a report which we submitted to the government of the USSR on the request of the Russian Command of the Concentration Camp for Italian ex-prisoners at Kattowitz. We were inmates of this Camp ourselves after our

Published in *Minerva Medica* (Turin), 37, 47 (24 November 1946): a weekly gazette for the medical practitioner.

liberation by the Red Army towards the end of January 1945. We have added some information of a general nature to the account given here, since our original report was required to concentrate exclusively on the operation of medical services in the Monowitz Camp. Similar reports were requested by the government in Moscow from all doctors, of whatever nationality, who had been liberated in the same way from other Camps.

We left the Concentration Camp at Fossoli di Carpi (Modena) on 22 February 1944 with a convoy of 650 Jews of both sexes and all ages. The oldest was over 80, the youngest a baby of 3 months. Many were ill, and some seriously so: an old man of 70 who had been struck down by a cerebral haemorrhage a few days before our departure was loaded onto the train anyway and died during the journey.

The train consisted simply of cattle trucks, locked on the outside; every wagon was crammed with over fifty people, the majority of whom had brought as much luggage with them as they could, because a German warrant officer attached to the Fossoli Camp had suggested to us, with the air of giving a piece of disinterested and kindly advice, that we should provide ourselves with plenty of warm clothes – jerseys, rugs, fur coats – because we were going to be taken to lands with a much harsher climate than our own. And he had added, with a benevolent little smile and a knowing wink, that if anyone had any hidden money or jewellery on them then it would be a good idea to take that along as well, since it would certainly come in useful up there. Most of those who were leaving had risen to the bait and followed a piece of advice which concealed a crude trap; others, a very few, preferred to entrust their belongings to some private citizen with free access to the Camp; while still others, whose arrest had not given them time to provide themselves with a change of clothing, left with only what they had on their backs.

The journey from Fossoli to Auschwitz lasted for exactly four days, and it was a very painful one, particularly on account of the cold, which was so intense, especially during the night, that in the morning the metal pipes which ran along the insides of the trucks would be found covered with ice due to the condensation of water vapour from the air we had breathed out. Another torment was thirst, which could not be quenched except with the snow which we gathered on the single daily halt, when the convoy would stop in open countryside and the passengers were allowed to get out of the trucks under the strictest of surveillance from the numerous soldiers, ready, with their sub-machine-guns constantly aimed, to open fire on anyone who showed signs of moving away from the train.

It was during these brief halts that food was distributed, truck by truck: bread, jam and cheese, but never water or anything else to drink. The possibility of sleep was reduced to a minimum, since the quantity of suitcases and bundles cluttering the floor did not allow anyone to settle into a comfortable position in which they could rest; instead, all the passengers had to be content to crouch down as best they could in a very small space. The floor of the trucks was always soaking wet, and no provision had been made to cover it even with a little straw.

As soon as the train reached Auschwitz (at about 9 p.m. on 26 February 1944), the trucks were rapidly cleared by a number of SS men armed with pistols and equipped with batons, and the passengers were forced to leave their suitcases, bundles and rugs alongside the train. The company was immediately divided into three groups: one of young and apparently able-bodied men, comprising ninety-five individuals; a second of women, also young – a meagre group made up of only twenty-nine people – and a third, the most numerous of all, of the children, the infirm and the old. And, while the first two were sent separately to different Camps, there is reason to believe that the third was taken straight to the gas chamber at Birkenau, and its members slaughtered that same evening.

The first group was taken to Monowitz, where there was a Concentration Camp administratively dependent on Auschwitz, and about 8 kilometres away from it, which had been set up towards the middle of 1942 in order to provide labour for the construction of the 'Buna-Werke' industrial complex, a subsidiary of IG Farbenindustrie. It housed 10–12,000 prisoners, even though its normal capacity was only 7–8,000 men. The majority of these were Jews of every nationality in Europe, while a small minority was made up of German and Polish criminals, Polish 'politicals', and 'saboteurs'.

The 'Buna-Werke', intended for the production on a vast scale of synthetic rubber, synthetic gasoline, dyestuffs and other by-products of coal, occupied a rectangular area of about 35 square kilometres. One of the entrances to this industrial zone, completely surrounded by high barbed-wire fences, was situated a few hundred metres from the Concentration Camp for Jews, and a short distance from this, and adjoining the periphery of the industrial zone, was a Concentration Camp for English prisoners-of-war, while farther away there were other Camps for civilian workers of various nationalities. We should add that the production cycle of the 'Buna-Werke' was never initiated; the starting date, originally fixed for August 1944, was repeatedly postponed because of air raids and sabotage by Polish civilian workers, right up to the evacuation of the district by the German army.

Monowitz was therefore a typical 'Arbeits-Lager'. Every morning, the entire population of the Camp – apart from the sick and the small labour force assigned to internal work – would file out in perfect ranks, to the sound of a band playing military marches and cheerful popular songs, to reach their places of work, up to 6 or 7 kilometres distant for some squads. The route would be covered at a rapid pace, almost at a run. Before the departure for work, and after returning from it, the daily ceremony of the roll-call would take place in a special square in the Lager, where all the prisoners had to stand in rigid formation, for between one and three hours, whatever the weather.

As soon as they arrived at the Camp, the group of ninety-five men was taken to the disinfection unit, where all of its members were immediately made to undress and then subjected to a total and painstaking depilation: head hair, beards and all other hair quickly fell away beneath scissors, razors and clippers. After which they were put into the shower room and locked up there until the following morning. Tired, hungry, thirsty, half-asleep, amazed by what they had already seen and worried about their immediate future, but anxious above all about the fate of the dear ones from whom they had been suddenly and brutally separated a few hours earlier, with their minds tormented by sombre and tragic forebodings, they had to spend the whole night standing up, with their feet in the water that trickled from the pipes and ran over the floor. Finally, at about six the following morning, they were subjected to a complete rub-down with a solution of lysol and then to a hot shower, after which the Camp clothes were handed out, and they were sent to get dressed in another large room, which they had to reach from the outside of the building, going out naked into the snow with their bodies still wet from their recent shower.

The winter outfit of the Monowitz prisoners consisted of a jacket, a pair of trousers, a cap and an overcoat of woollen cloth in broad stripes, plus a shirt, a pair of cotton underpants and a pair of foot-cloths, a pullover and a pair of boots with wooden soles. Many of the foot-cloths and the underpants had obviously been made out of the *tallit* – the sacred shawl with which Jews cover themselves during prayers – retrieved from the luggage of some of the deportees and made use of in this way as a mark of contempt.

By the month of April, when the cold, though less severe, had not yet gone, the thick clothing and pullovers would be withdrawn and trousers and jackets replaced by similar articles in cotton, also with broad stripes; and only towards the end of October would the winter garments be distributed again. However, this no longer happened in the autumn of '44 because the woollen suits and coats had reached the end of any possibility of reuse, so the prisoners had to face the winter of '44 to '45 dressed in the same thin clothes as during the summer months, with only a small minority being given a light gabardine raincoat or a pullover.

Having spare clothes or underwear was strictly forbidden, so it was practically impossible to wash shirts or underpants; these items were officially changed at intervals of thirty, forty or fifty days, depending on availability and without the possibility of choice. The new underwear was not actually clean, of course, but simply disinfected by steam, because there was no laundry in the Camp. It usually consisted of short cotton underpants and of shirts: always cotton or some other thin cloth, often without sleeves, always of a disgusting appearance because of the many stains of all kinds, and often reduced to rags. Sometimes instead one would be given the jacket or trousers from a pair of pyjamas, or even some article of female underwear. The repeated disinfections weakened the fibres of the cloth, removing all resistance to wear and tear.

All this material represented the shoddiest part of the linen seized from the members of the various transports which, as is common knowledge, flooded ceaselessly into the station at Auschwitz from every part of Europe. Coats, jackets and trousers, whether summer or winter, were distributed in an unbelievably bad condition, covered with patches and impregnated with filth (mud, machine oil, paint). The prisoners were personally obliged to see to repairs, although they were not provided with either needles or thread. Permission for an exchange was obtained with extreme difficulty, and only when any attempt at repair was clearly impossible. Footcloths could not be exchanged at all, and their replacement was left to the initiative of each individual. It was forbidden to own a handkerchief, or indeed a scrap of cloth of any kind.

The boots were made in a special workshop inside the Camp; the wooden soles were nailed to uppers of leather, leatherette, or cloth and rubber, taken from the shoddiest of the footwear obtained from incoming convoys. When they were in good condition they provided reasonable protection against the cold and the wet, but they were completely unsuitable for marches, however short, and were the cause of epidermal ulcers of the feet. Anyone in possession of boots that were the right size and a matching pair could count himself lucky. When they deteriorated they were repaired innumerable times, beyond any reasonable limit, so new footwear was very rarely seen, and the sort usually handed out did not last for more than a week. Bootlaces were not distributed and substitutes were contrived by each individual from twisted paper cord, or from electric flex when it was possible to find any.

Hygienic and sanitary conditions in the Camp actually appeared at first sight to be good: the paths and avenues that separated the various 'blocks' were well maintained and clean, in so far as the mud of the road surface permitted; the outsides of the 'blocks' were of well-painted wood, and the insides had floors diligently swept and washed every morning, with the three-storey bunks, the so-called 'castles', perfectly aligned and the blankets on the pallets completely flat and smooth. But all this was only the outward appearance; the reality was very different – in fact, the 'blocks', which should normally have housed 150 to 170 people, were always crammed with no fewer than 200, and often as many as 250, so that 2 people had to sleep in almost every bed. In these conditions, the cubic capacity of the dormitory was certainly less than the minimum needed for respiration and oxygenation of the blood. The pallets consisted of a sort of palliasse more or less filled with wood-shavings, reduced almost to dust from long use, and of two blankets. Apart from the fact that these were never changed, and not subjected, except very rarely and for exceptional reasons, to any disinfection, they were mostly in a dreadful state: threadbare from very long use, torn and covered in stains of every kind. Only the pallets most in view were provided with more decent covers, almost clean and sometimes even attractive; these were the pallets on the lower tiers and nearest the entrance door.

Naturally these beds were reserved for the minor 'hierarchs' of the Camp: the squad Kapos and their assistants, the aides of the block Kapo, or simply the friends of one or other of these.

This explains the impression of cleanliness, order and hygiene which greeted anyone entering a dormitory for the first time and giving the inside a superficial glance. In the structure of the 'castles', the supporting beams and the planks on which the pallets rested, lived thousands of bed bugs and fleas which gave the prisoners sleepless nights; nor were the disinfections of the dormitories with nitrogen mustard vapour, which were carried out every three or four months, sufficient for the destruction of these guests, which continued to vegetate and multiply almost undisturbed.

Against lice, on the other hand, a war to the death was waged in order to avert the onset of an epidemic of petechial typhus; every evening on returning from work, and with greater strictness on Saturday afternoons (devoted, among other things, to the shaving of heads and beards, and sometimes also of body hair) the so-called 'louse inspection' would be carried out. Every prisoner had to strip and subject his garments to a meticulous examination by the specially appointed inspectors, and if even a single louse was found on a deportee's shirt, all the personal clothing of every inmate of the dormitory was immediately despatched to be disinfected, and the men were subjected to a shower, preceded by a rub-down with lysol. They then had to spend the entire night naked, until their clothes were brought back from the disinfection hut in the early hours of the morning, soaking wet.

However, no other prophylactic measures were put in place against infectious diseases, even though there was no shortage of these: typhus and scarlet fever, diphtheria and chickenpox, measles, erysipelas, etc., not counting the numerous skin infections, such as tineas, impetigo and scabies. It is quite astonishing, given such disregard for the rules of hygiene and with people living in such close proximity, that rapidly spreading epidemics never broke out.

One of the greatest risk factors for the transmission of infectious diseases was represented by the fact that a significant percentage of prisoners were not provided with a mess tin or a spoon; consequently, three or four people in succession would be forced to eat from the same container or with the same implement, without having had the chance to wash it.

The food, inadequate in quantity, was of inferior quality. It consisted of three meals: in the morning, straight after reveille, 350 grams of bread would be distributed on four days of the week and 700 grams on the other three, giving a daily average of 500 grams – an amount which would have been fairly reasonable if the bread itself had not indisputably contained a very large quantity of dross, amongst which sawdust was much in evidence; also in the mornings, there would be 25 grams of margarine with about 20 grams of sausage or a spoonful of jam or soft cheese. The margarine was distributed on six days of the week only, and later this was reduced to three. At noon the deportees received a litre of turnip or cabbage soup, completely tasteless due to the absence of any kind of flavouring, and every evening after work a further litre of a slightly thicker soup with a few potatoes or now and then some peas and chickpeas, but this too was completely devoid of any fat to flavour it. One might infrequently find a few shreds of meat. To drink, half a litre of ersatz coffee, without sugar, was distributed morning and evening; only on Sundays was it sweetened with saccharin. There was no drinking water at Monowitz; the running water in the washrooms could only be put to external use, since it was river water, which arrived at the Camp neither filtered nor sterilized and was therefore highly dubious. It was clear in appearance, but of a yellowish colour if seen in any depth; its taste was between the metallic and the sulphurous.

The prisoners were required to take a shower two or three times a week. However, these ablutions were not sufficient to keep them clean as soap was handed out in very parsimonious quantities: only a single 50-gram bar per month. Its quality was extremely poor; it consisted of a rectangular block, very hard, devoid of any fatty material but instead full of sand. It did not produce lather and disintegrated very easily, so that after a couple of showers it was completely used up. After showering, there was no way of rubbing down one's body or of drying it since there were no towels, and on coming out of the bath-house one had to run naked, whatever the time of year, the atmospheric and meteorological conditions, or the temperature, as far as one's own particular 'block', where one's clothes had been left.

The work to which the great majority of prisoners was assigned was manual labour of various kinds, all very demanding and unsuited to the physical condition and the abilities of those condemned to it; very few were employed in work which had any connection with the profession or trade they had practised in civilian life. Thus, neither of the present writers were able to work in the hospital or in the chemical laboratory of the 'Buna-Werke', but were forced to share the lot of their companions and undergo labours beyond their strength, sometimes working as navvies with pick and shovel, sometimes unloading coal or sacks of cement, or doing other sorts of very heavy work, all of which naturally took place out of doors, winter and summer, in snow, rain, sun or wind, and without clothing that provided adequate protection against low temperatures or bad weather. This kind of work, moreover, always had to be carried out at the double and without any breaks except for an hour, from noon till one, for the midday meal; woe betide anyone who was caught being inactive or standing at ease during working hours.

From the brief account we have given of living conditions in the Monowitz Concentration Camp, it is easy to deduce the diseases which most frequently affected the prisoners, along with their causes. They can be divided into the following groups:

(1) dystrophic diseases
(2) diseases of the gastrointestinal apparatus
(3) diseases due to cold
(4) infectious diseases, general and cutaneous
(5) conditions requiring surgery
(6) work-related conditions.

Dystrophic diseases – The diet, which, as we have seen, was much inferior to what was required from a quantitative point of view, was lacking from a qualitative one in two important respects: it was deficient, that is to say, in fats, and especially in animal protein, apart from those miserable 20–25 grams of sausage that were provided two or three times a week. It was also lacking in vitamins. It is clear, therefore, that nutritional deficiencies of these kinds and on this scale were the primary cause of the dystrophies that affected almost all of the prisoners from their first weeks as inmates. All of them, in fact, very quickly became emaciated, and the majority of them presented with oedemas, particularly localized to the lower limbs, although oedemas of the face were also present. These dystrophies can also be held responsible for the ease with which various infections were contracted, especially those affecting the integrity of the skin, and for their tendency to become chronic. Thus, certain epidermal ulcers of the feet, directly caused by the footwear, which was anti-physiological in shape and size; boils, which were very frequent and numerous in the same subject; the equally frequent leg ulcers; phlegmons, etc., would not show any tendency to heal but would turn into turbid sores with a lardaceous base and continual seropurulent suppuration, and sometimes with an abundance of yellowish-grey granulomas which were not ameliorated even by painting with silver nitrate. And finally, the diarrhoea that affected almost all of the deportees can also be attributed, to a significant extent, to alimentary dystrophy. This explains why the deportees rapidly lost their strength, since the disappearance of subcutaneous fat was accompanied by the onset of considerable atrophy of the muscular tissue.

At this point we need to mention vitamins. From what we have reported so far, it might seem obvious that vitamin deficiency syndromes – particularly from the lack of vitamin

C and vitamin B – would be common. On the contrary, as far
as we are aware, cases of scurvy or polyneuritis did not occur,
at least in a typical and fully developed form, and we believe
this to be due to the fact that the average life expectancy of
the majority of prisoners was too short for the body to have
time to display obvious clinical symptoms of suffering from
the lack of those vitamins.

Diseases of the gastrointestinal apparatus – We will pass
over those diseases, by which many prisoners were affected,
which were not directly caused by living conditions in the
Camp, such as low or high stomach acid, gastro-duodenal
ulcers, appendicitis, inflammation of the bowel, diseases of
the liver. We will note only that these pathological conditions, pre-existent in many deportees before their arrival at
Monowitz, became aggravated, or underwent relapses if previously cured. What we particularly want to discuss here is
the diarrhoea to which we have already referred in the previous paragraph, both because of its prevalence and because
of the gravity of its course, in many cases rapidly fatal. It
usually erupted suddenly, sometimes preceded by dyspep-
tic disturbances, as a result of some immediate cause that
represented the accidental determining factor, such as, for
example, a prolonged exposure to cold or the consumption of
food which had gone bad (sometimes the bread was mouldy)
or which was difficult to digest. It is worth mentioning in
this connection that many prisoners, to relieve the pangs of
hunger, would eat potato peelings, raw cabbage leaves or
rotten potatoes or turnips which they collected from amongst
the kitchen refuse. However, it is probable that there were
many other causal factors in serious cases of diarrhoea, and
two interdependent ones in particular: chronic dyspepsia and
the resulting dystrophy due to malnutrition. Those affected
presented with numerous evacuations of the bowels – from
a minimum of five or six up to twenty or even more a day
– liquid and with a great deal of mucus, sometimes accompanied by blood, and preceded and accompanied by acute
abdominal pain. The appetite might be preserved, but in
many cases the patients presented with persistent anorexia,
so that they refused to take any nourishment; these were the
most serious cases, which rapidly developed towards a fatal
outcome. There was invariably a very intense thirst. If the

condition showed a tendency towards recovery, the number of evacuations diminished, becoming reduced to two or three a day, while the consistency of the faeces altered, becoming less liquid. From these bouts of diarrhoea the patients always emerged in poor condition, with a considerable worsening of their general state of health and a more pronounced appearance of emaciation due to the significant dehydration of the tissues. The standardized treatment was two-fold: nutritional and medicinal. Having been admitted to hospital, the patients were subjected to a total fast for a period of 24 hours, after which they were given a special diet until their condition had decidedly improved: that is until, the number of evacuations having diminished and the faeces having become more formed, the prognosis of their illness had become clearly favourable. This dietary regime consisted in the suspension of the sausage ration and the midday soup; black bread was replaced by white and the evening soup by sweetened semolina, reasonably thick. In addition, the doctors advised the patients to drink little liquid, or preferably not to drink at all, although the quantity of morning and evening coffee was not officially reduced. Medicinal treatment was based on the administration of three or four albumin tannate tablets and the same number of charcoal tablets 'pro die'; in the most serious cases, the patients also received five drops (!) of tincture of opium together with a few drops of cardiazol.

Diseases due to cold – The daily prolonged exposure to the cold and to harsh weather, against which the prisoners were not protected in any way, and to the wet, explains the frequency of rheumatic conditions affecting the respiratory system and the joints, of neuralgias and of frostbite.

Bronchitis, pneumonia and broncho-pneumonia were, so to speak, the order of the day even during the summer, but naturally they were particularly rampant during the winter, autumn and spring. Treatment was extremely basic: cold compresses on the chest, a few antipyretic tablets and, in the most serious cases, sulphonamides in totally inadequate doses, along with a little cardiazol. For neuralgias – lumbago and sciatica were especially common – and for arthritis, the patients were subjected to heat treatment; no treatment was practised for frostbite apart from amputation of the affected part when the frostbite was sufficiently severe.

Infectious diseases – The exanthemata represented the most common of these, especially scarlet fever, chickenpox, erysipelas and diphtheria. Cases of abdominal typhus also occurred from time to time. Anyone who came down with one of these diseases would be admitted to an isolation ward, but in an indiscriminate way: without, that is, there being any separation between patients with different kinds of infection. Consequently, it was very easy for a patient who had been admitted to the infirmary with one infectious disease to contract another there through contagion, especially since neither the blankets on the beds nor the bowls in which the soup was distributed were ever disinfected. Scarlet fever and erysipelas were combatted with sulphonamides – always administered, however, in reduced doses; diphtheria cases were left to themselves due to the total lack of serum, and their treatment was limited to gargling with a very dilute solution of chinosol and to the administration of a few Panflavin lozenges. Understandably, the death rate for diphtheria was 100%, since any patients who managed to survive the acute phase succumbed later to cardiac arrest, either because of some further complication or because they also came down with another contagious disease.

As to syphilis, tuberculosis and malaria, we are not able to give any data as to their frequency since the syphilitic, the tubercular and the malarial – the latter even if long since cured and accidentally found out through their own incautious confession – were immediately dispatched to Birkenau and eliminated there in the gas chambers. It cannot be denied that this was a radical prophylactic method!

Skin infections of every kind were very prevalent, but especially boils and abscesses – which, as we have already said, always had a very protracted course, subject to relapses and with many concurrent sites – as well as sycosis of the beard area and tineas. Against the former, only surgical treatment by incision and drainage was carried out, since there was no possibility of practising fever therapy by means of vaccine or drug treatment – although, in the most persistent cases, the patients were subjected to autohemotherapy. Against the latter – sycosis and tineas – there were no specific remedies, and in particular no iodine. The sufferers' faces were plastered with one or another of the available ointments, with less than no therapeutic effect. In the light of the ever greater prevalence of these skin diseases, on the one hand such prophylactic measures as a ban on patients having their beards shaved, to prevent the transmission of infection by razors and shaving-brushes, were finally adopted, while, on the other, steps were taken to intensify treatment by subjecting the patients to ultraviolet radiation. The most serious cases of sycosis were temporarily transferred to the hospital at Auschwitz to undergo X-ray therapy.

On the subject of skin conditions, we must once again mention the prevalence of scabies, which was treated with a daily rub-down with mitigal in a special ward to which patients were admitted only in the evenings, spending the nights there while having to continue working during the day in the squad to which they were normally attached. In other words, there was no special 'Kommando' for scabies sufferers to which those infested were assigned for the duration of their condition; so, since they continued to work in the midst of individuals who had not yet been infested, contagion was very frequent, due to the shared use of tools and to living in close proximity.

Conditions requiring surgery – Once again we do not wish to dwell on conditions requiring surgical intervention which were not causally connected to living conditions in the Camp. We will simply report that even major surgery was regularly performed, mostly abdominal, such as partial gastrectomy and pyloroplasty for gastro-duodenal ulcers, appendectomies, rib resections for empyema, etc.; as well as orthopaedic interventions for fractures and dislocations. If the general condition of the patient did not offer sufficient guarantee of resistance to the trauma of surgery, he would be given a blood transfusion before the operation; this was also done to combat anaemia secondary to serious haemorrhages caused by gastric ulcers or accidental trauma. For donors, recourse was had to recently arrived deportees who were still in good general shape; blood donation was voluntary and the donor was rewarded with a fortnight's rest in hospital, during which time he received special rations. For this reason, offers of blood were always very numerous.

We have no reason to suppose – indeed, we believe that we can rule it out – that operations for the purpose of scientific research were performed in the Monowitz hospital, as they were on a vast scale in other Concentration Camps. We know, for example, that at Auschwitz a section of the hospital was used for research into the effects of castration followed by cross-gender grafting of the reproductive glands.

The operating theatre was reasonably well equipped, in so far as was necessary for the procedures carried out there. The walls were covered in washable white tiles; there was an adjustable operating table, of a rather old-fashioned type but still in good condition, which allowed the patient to be placed in the main operative positions, and an electric steril-izer for surgical instruments; illumination was provided by several movable lamps and a large, fixed, central light. On one wall, behind a wooden screen, wash-basins with hot and cold running water were installed so that the surgeon and his assistants could scrub their hands.

On the subject of aseptic surgery, we should add that hernias were also regularly operated on at the request of the patient, at least until the middle of spring 1944; from then on these operations were discontinued – apart from very exceptional cases of strangulated hernia – even when it was a question of very large hernias that were really an impediment to work. This decision was taken on the supposition that patients might submit themselves to the operation in order to get a month's rest in hospital.

The most frequent operations were for phlegmons, and were carried out in a theatre set aside for surgery dealing with septic conditions. Phlegmons, along with diarrhoea, consti-tuted one of the most important chapters in the characteristic pathology of the Concentration Camp. They were mainly localized on the lower limbs, more rarely having their site in some other part of the body. As a rule, it was possible to identify their starting-point in cutaneous lesions of the feet, caused by the footwear: ulcers, originally superficial and of limited extent, which became infected and spread, with locally extending infiltration, either peripheral or in depth, or giving rise to metastatic infiltration at a distance. At times, though, it was not possible to determine the point of entry of the pathogenic micro-organisms, the infiltration of the soft tissue having developed without it being possible to detect any cutaneous lesion in its vicinity or at a distance; this was probably due to a localization of micro-organisms originating in some focus from which they had been transferred via the bloodstream. Patients were operated on without delay, with numerous ample incisions; however, the subsequent development of the lesions was always very lengthy and, even when suppuration was coming to an end, the incisions did not show any tendency to scar over. Post-operative treatment consisted simply in drainage of the surgical wound; no treatment was put into effect to stimulate the body's own defences. Relapses were therefore very likely, leading to a succession of operations on the same individual to open and drain the sacs of pus that formed at the periphery of the previous incisions. When eventually the healing process appeared to have reached a satisfactory stage, patients would be discharged from hospital and sent back to work even though their wounds had not yet completely healed, and subsequent treatment was carried out on an out-patient basis. It stands to reason that the majority of those discharged in this way had to return to hospital after a few days, either because of local relapses or due to the development of new foci in other sites.

Also very common was acute otitis, which led to a particularly high percentage of mastoid complications; these too were routinely operated on by the otorhinolaryngologist.

The treatment of skin infections was based on the use of four ointments, which were applied successively in a standardized way, depending on the stage of the lesions. Firstly, at the infiltration stage, the lesion and the surrounding skin were covered with ichthyol ointment to reduce swelling; later, once the formation of pus had occurred and the focus had been opened, its base was covered with collargol ointment as a disinfectant; once the suppuration had ceased or greatly diminished, pellidol ointment was used to stimulate scar formation, followed by another of zinc oxide to aid epithelialization.

Work-related conditions – Given the very high rate of employment in manual labour, specific occupational diseases were not really in evidence apart from accidental injuries requiring surgery, such as contusions, fractures and dislocations; but we can report on one case which is known to us.

At a certain period – August 1944 – the men attached to the so-called 'Chemical Commando' were employed in reorganizing a storeroom containing sacks of a substance of a phenolic nature. From the very first day of work, this substance, in the form of fine powder, stuck to the faces and hands of the labourers, held there by their sweat; subsequent exposure to the sun caused, in all of them, first a strong pigmentation of the exposed areas, accompanied by intense burning, and then an extensive desquamation in large flakes. Even though the new layer of skin that was thus exposed to the contaminating agent was particularly sensitive and painful, the work continued for three weeks without any protective measures being adopted. And even though all of the men in the above-mentioned Commando – about fifty of them – were affected by this painful dermatitis, none of them was admitted to hospital.

Having given this survey of the most common diseases in the Monowitz Camp and of their causes, we are forced to admit that we are unable to give precise data on their frequency in absolute and relative terms, since neither of us ever had the chance to enter the hospital except as a patient. What we have written so far, and what we still have to say, is the fruit of everyday observation and of the information which we gleaned more or less accidentally while conversing with our companions and with doctors and infirmary staff with whom we were on terms of familiarity or friendship.

The Camp hospital was set up only a few months before our arrival at Monowitz, which took place towards the end of February 1944. Before that period, there were no medical services and the sick had no possibility of getting treatment, but were forced to labour as usual every day until they collapsed from exhaustion at their work. Naturally, such cases occurred with great frequency. Confirmation of death would then be carried out in a singular fashion; the task was entrusted to two individuals, not doctors, who were armed with ox sinews and had to beat the fallen man for several minutes without stopping. After they had finished, if he failed to react with some movement, he was considered to be dead, and his body was immediately taken to the crematory. If, on the contrary, he moved, it signified that he was not dead after all, so he would be forced to resume his interrupted work.

Later on, the basic nucleus of a medical service was established, with the setting-up of an out-patient clinic, where anyone who felt ill could present himself for a medical examination – although, if someone was not recognized as ill by the doctors, he would immediately receive severe corporal punishment from the SS. Otherwise, if his condition was judged to be such as to prevent him from working, he would be granted a few days' rest. Later still, a few blocks were set aside for use as an infirmary, which gradually expanded with the setting-up of additional services; so that, during our stay in the Camp, the following were in operation:

- out-patient clinic for general medicine
- out-patient clinic for general surgery
- otorhinolaryngology and ophthalmology out-patient clinic
- dental surgery (in which fillings and the most basic prosthetic work were also carried out)
- ward for septic surgery cases
- general clinical ward, with a section for nervous and mental illnesses, equipped with a small electric shock therapy apparatus
- ward for infectious diseases and diarrhoea
- recuperation ward – 'Schonungs-Block' – to which were admitted dystrophic and oedematous patients and certain convalescents
- physiotherapy surgery, with a quartz lamp for ultraviolet radiation and lamps for infrared radiation
- chemical, bacteriological and serological research unit.

There were no X-ray machines, so if an X-ray examination was needed the patient would be dispatched to Auschwitz, where there was good X-ray equipment, and from where he would return with a radiological diagnosis.

This description might suggest a hospital which was small, certainly, but complete in almost every department and efficiently run; but in reality there were many deficiencies, some of which, such as the lack of drugs and the shortage of medical equipment, were perhaps insurmountable, given the grave situation in which Germany already found herself, under pressure on one side from the unstoppable advance of the brave Russian troops and on the other from daily air raids by the heroic Anglo-American air force; but others could have been remedied, had there been the will to do so, by better organization of services.

The first and most important of these deficiencies was the inadequacy in number and capacity of the facilities. For example, there was no waiting-room for the clinics, so patients reporting to them were forced to stay out of doors, awaiting their turn in endless queues, whatever the season and whatever the weather, when, already exhausted from their long working day, they returned to the Camp in the evening – since the out-patient facilities were only in operation after all the labourers had returned to the Camp and the evening roll-call was over. Before entering the clinics, every patient had to take off his shoes, and was therefore forced to walk with bare feet over floors, such as that of the surgical out-patient clinic, which were very dirty due to the presence of used dressings thrown on the ground, and consequently soiled with blood and pus.

In the wards, there was a very serious shortage in the number of beds, which made it necessary for every pallet to be used by two people, whatever the nature and the gravity of the disease from which they were suffering; the possibility of contagion was therefore very high, especially considering the fact that, due to the lack of shirts, the hospital patients went naked; indeed, on entry to the hospital, every patient would deposit all his clothes in the disinfection unit. The blankets and palliasses of the pallets were absolutely filthy, stained with blood and pus and often with faeces, which patients in a pre-agonal state would void involuntarily.

The rules of hygiene were completely ignored, apart from what little was necessary to keep up appearances. So, for example, due to a shortage of mess tins, meals would be served in two or three shifts, and the patients in the second or third shift would be forced to eat their soup from receptacles inadequately rinsed in a bucket of cold water. In the so-called 'Schonungs-Block', running water had not been plumbed in, as was indeed the case in all the other wards; but while the inmates of the latter were able to go to a specially designated 'Waschraum' to wash themselves whenever they wanted, those admitted to the former were only able to avail themselves of the chance to wash once a day, in the morning, with over 200 of them sharing six basins into which the nurses would occasionally pour a litre of water from tubs brought in for this purpose from outside. In this same ward, the bread would be brought in from the dressing station, where it had been left the previous evening on a bench which, during the day, served the patients as a stool on which to prop their feet while their dressings were being changed, after which it was always smeared with blood and pus, which would then be hastily wiped off with a rag soaked in cold water.

In order to be allowed into the hospital, the patients judged by the clinic doctors to be worthy of admission had to report a second time the following morning, immediately after reveille, to undergo another, very cursory examination by the doctor in charge of medical services; if he confirmed the need for hospitalization, they would be sent to the shower room. There they would be shaved to the last hair, then made to take a shower, and finally they would be sent to the relevant section of the hospital. To get there, they would have to go outside, covered only by a wrap, and walk 100–200 metres in this state, whatever the season and whatever the atmospheric and meteorological conditions.

In the various clinical wards, the doctor in charge, assisted by one or two nurses, would perform his morning round without personally going up to the patients' beds; rather, it was they who would have to get out of bed and go to him, excluding only those who were completely prevented from doing so by the seriousness of their condition. In the evenings, there would be a rapid follow-up examination.

In the surgical wards, the dressings would be applied in the mornings, and, since the dormitory was divided into three aisles and each aisle was treated in turn, it followed that each patient received treatment only every third day. The dressings were secured with paper bandages which tore and came apart in the course of a few hours; so the wounds, whether septic or not, were always left exposed. Only in rare and exceptional cases would dressings be secured with adhesive plaster, which was used with the utmost frugality on account of its scarcity.

Medication was reduced to a minimum; many products, even the most basic and commonly used, were totally absent, while of others there was only a meagre amount. There was a little aspirin, a little pyramidon, a little prontosil (the only representative of the sulphonamides), a little sodium bicarbonate, a few phials of coramine and caffeine. There was no camphorated oil, no strychnine, no opium or any of its derivatives apart from a small quantity of tincture; there was no belladonna or atropine; there was no insulin, no expectorants, nor yet salts of bismuth or Epsom salts, pepsin or hydrochloric acid, while the purgatives and laxatives were represented only by purgatin. However, there were reasonable quantities of hexamethylenetetramine, of medicinal charcoal and of albumin tannate. Also missing were phials of calcium and of any preparation which would act as a tonic. There was a reasonable quantity of soluble evipal for intravenous use and of phials of ethyl chloride for anaesthesia; the latter was widely used even for minor interventions, such as lancing a boil.

Every so often, the dispensary was given new blood by the receipt, on the arrival of new convoys of prisoners, of various quantities of the most disparate products and the most diverse proprietary drugs, many of them useless, discovered in the luggage confiscated from the new arrivals; but, all in all, requirements were always far in excess of supply.

The staff were recruited entirely from among the deportees themselves. The doctors were chosen, subject to examination, from among those who had declared on entering the Camp that they had a degree in medicine, with priority going to those who were fluent in German or Polish. Their services were rewarded with improved rations and better clothing and footwear. The orderlies and nurses, on the other hand, were picked without any criterion of previous professional experience; for the most part they were striking physical specimens who had obtained their positions – naturally very much sought after – thanks to their friendships and connections with doctors already in post, or with members of the hierarchy of the Camp. It followed that, while the doctors, on the whole, displayed a reasonable competence and a certain degree of civility, the auxiliary staff distinguished themselves by their ignorance of, or contempt for, every hygienic, therapeutic and humanitarian principle; they went so far as to barter part of the soup and bread intended for the patients in exchange for cigarettes, items of clothing and other things. The patients were often beaten for trivial offences; the distribution of rations took place in an irregular way, and when it came to prisoners who were found guilty of more serious faults – such as stealing bread from their companions – the customary punishment was the immediate expulsion of the culprit from the hospital, and his immediate return to work, preceded by the administration of a certain number of blows (usually twenty-five) to the back, delivered very energetically with a tube of rubberized cloth. Another type of punishment was being forced to spend a quarter of an hour on a rather high stool with a very narrow seat, balancing on tip-toe, with the legs bent at the knees and hips and the arms held out horizontally in front at shoulder height. Usually the patient would lose his balance after a few minutes because of muscular fatigue and bodily weakness and tumble to the ground, to the great entertainment of the nurses, who would make a circle round him, mocking him with jeers and gibes. The fallen man would have to get up, re-ascend the stool and take up his position again for the allotted time; if, because of successive falls, he was no longer capable of doing so, the remainder of the punishment would be made up with a certain number of lashes.

The influx of patients was always very great, far in excess of the capacity of the various wards, so to make room for the new arrivals a certain number of patients would be discharged every day, even if not completely recovered and still in a state of serious general debility – despite which, they would have to start work again the following day. But those suffering from chronic diseases, or whose stay in hospital had lasted longer than a period of about two months, or who were readmitted too often due to relapses of their illness, were sent – as we have already reported in the case of those with tuberculosis, syphilis or malaria – to Birkenau and there eliminated in the gas chambers. The same fate was suffered by those too depleted to be able to work. Every so often – about once a month – the so-called 'selection of the Muslims' (this picturesque term denoted precisely these extremely emaciated individuals) took place in the various wards of the hospital, with the most physically broken-down being singled out to be dispatched to the gas chambers. These selections were conducted with great rapidity and were carried out by the doctor in charge of medical services, in front of whom all the patients filed naked, while he judged the general condition of each one with a superficial glance, instantly deciding their fate. A few days later, those selected underwent a second examination by a medical captain in the SS who was the director general of medical services in all the Camps subsidiary to Auschwitz. It has to be admitted that this inspection was more thorough than the previous one, with each case being weighed up and discussed; at all events, it was only a lucky few who were removed from the list and readmitted to hospital for further treatment or sent to some Commando where the work was regarded as light; the majority were condemned to death. One of us was included in the list of 'Muslims' no fewer than four times, and escaped each time from a fatal outcome, thanks simply to the fact of being a doctor, since – we do not know whether as a general rule or through an initiative on the part of the administration of the Monowitz Camp – doctors were spared from such a fate.

In October 1944, the selection, instead of being restricted to the wards of the hospital, was extended to all the 'blocks'; but this was the last one, since after that date this kind of exercise was discontinued and the gas chambers at Birkenau were demolished. Nevertheless, 850 victims were selected during that tragic day, among them 8 Jews of Italian nationality.

The work of operating the gas chambers and the adjacent crematory was carried out by a special Commando which worked day and night, in two shifts. The members of this Commando lived in isolation, carefully segregated from any contact with other prisoners or with the outside world. Their clothes gave off a sickening stench, they were always filthy and they had an utterly savage appearance, just like wild animals. They were picked from amongst the worst criminals, convicted of serious and bloody crimes.

It appears that in February 1943 a new crematory oven and gas chamber were inaugurated at Birkenau, more functional than those which had been in operation up to that month. These consisted of three areas: the waiting room, the 'shower room', and the ovens. At the centre of the ovens rose a tall chimney, around which were nine ovens with four openings each, all of them allowing the passage of three corpses at a time. The capacity of each oven was 2,000 corpses a day.

The victims would be ushered into the first room and ordered to undress completely, because – they were told – they had got to take a shower. To make the foul deception more credible, they were handed a piece of soap and a towel, after which they were made to enter the 'shower room'. This was a very large room equipped with fake shower fittings, and with conspicuous signs on the walls saying things like 'Wash thoroughly, because cleanliness is health', 'Don't economize on soap', 'Remember not to leave your towel here!', so as to make the place look just like a large public bath-house. In the flat ceiling of the room there was a large aperture, hermetically closed by three big metal plates that opened with a valve. A set of rails traversed the whole breadth of the chamber, leading from it to the ovens. When everyone had entered the gas chamber, the doors would be locked (they were airtight) and a chemical preparation in the form of a coarse powder, blue-grey in colour, would be dropped through the valve in the ceiling. It was in metal containers whose labels read 'Zyklon B – For the destruction of all kinds of vermin', and carried the trade mark of a factory in Hamburg. In fact, it was a preparation of cyanide which evaporated at a certain temperature. In the course of a few minutes, all those locked into the gas chamber would die; and then the doors and windows would be flung open, and the members of the Special Commando, equipped with gas masks, would enter in order to take the corpses to the crematory ovens.

Before putting the bodies into the ovens, a specially designated squad would cut off the hair of those who still had it – that is, from the corpses of those who, as soon as they arrived with their transports, were immediately taken to be slaughtered without entering the Camps; and they also extracted the gold teeth from those who had them. The ashes, it is well known, were then scattered in fields and vegetable gardens as a fertilizer for the soil.

Towards the end of 1944, orders reached the Monowitz Camp that all the doctors present in the Camp were to be released from working in the Commandos and employed in the various sections of the hospital, as doctors or, in the absence of available posts, as nurses. Before being assigned to their new duties, they had to spend a month gaining experience in the various clinical and surgical departments, following a certain rota, and at the same time they had to

take a theoretical training course on the medical organization of the Concentration Camps and how they were run, the
characteristic pathology of the Camps and the treatments to
be practised on the patients. These orders were duly carried
out and the course began in early January 1945; but towards
the middle of the same month it was broken off due to the
overwhelming Russian offensive in the Kraców-Kattowitz-
Wrocław direction, in the face of which the German forces
gave themselves up to headlong flight. The Monowitz Camp
was evacuated, along with all the others in the region of
Auschwitz, and the Germans dragged about 11,000 prisoners along with them, who, according to information received
later from someone who made a miraculous escape, were
almost all slaughtered by bursts of machine-gun fire a few
days later, when the soldiers escorting them realized that
they were completely surrounded by the Red Army and so no
longer had any way open to retreat. They had already travelled some 70 kilometres on foot, almost without stopping
and with no food, since the provisions they received before
leaving the Camp had consisted only of a kilogram of bread,
75 grams of margarine, 90 grams of sausage and 45 of sugar.
Later they had been loaded onto a number of trains which,
though taking a number of different routes, were unable to
reach any destination. The massacre then took place of the
survivors of such superhuman exertions; many – perhaps
3,000 or 4,000 – who had stopped on the road, overcome
by fatigue, had already been butchered on the spot by pistol
shots or by the gun-butts of the soldiers escorting them.

Meanwhile, only about 1,000 incapacitated, sick or convalescent prisoners who were unable to walk had been left
in the Camp, under the surveillance of a few SS men who
had been ordered to shoot them before leaving. We do not
know why this final order was not carried out, but, whatever
the reason may have been, it is to this alone that the present
writers owe the fact that they are still alive. They had been
kept back in the hospital, one detailed to give medical aid
to the patients and the other because he was convalescent.
The order to take care of the patients could not be carried
out except in terms of moral support, since material aid was
rendered impossible by the fact that, before abandoning the
Camp, the Germans had the hospital stripped of every drug

and every surgical instrument; there was no longer so much as an aspirin tablet, a pair of forceps or a gauze dressing.

There followed some highly dramatic days; many patients died from lack of treatment, and many from depletion, since there was also a lack of food. The water mains had been destroyed in an air raid which took place just at this time, so there was no water either. Only the chance discovery of a cache of potatoes, buried in a nearby field to protect them from frost, enabled the least enfeebled to feed themselves and to hold out until the day the Russians finally arrived and made generous provision for the distribution of food.

2

Record by Dr Primo Levi, Registration No. 174517, Survivor of Monowitz-Buna

Primo Levi

[1945]

Out of the Italian Jews deported to Germany at various times, there were about forty people surviving in the Buna camp at the beginning of January 1945.

On 17 January the camp SS suddenly received orders to transport to Germany all the internees of the camp (whether Jewish or not) who were capable of walking.

The text, three typed pages without signature or date, was found in Turin in the Archivio delle Tradizioni e del Costume Ebraici 'Benvenuto e Alessandro Terracini' (Benvenuto and Alessandro Terracini Archive of Jewish Traditions and Customs). It can be dated to the final weeks of 1945 – that is to say, shortly after Levi's return from deportation, which took place on 19 October.

Among the names on the list, the reader of *If This is a Man* will discover several familiar figures: Jean, the 'Pikolo' of the 'Canto of Ulysses' chapter; Alberto, Levi's friend in so many shared ventures; the engineer Aldo Levi, father of Emilia, the little girl sent to the gas chamber on arrival in the Lager (the chapter 'The Journey'); Clausner, who had scratched the words 'Ne pas chercher à comprendre' on the bottom of his mess tin (the chapter 'Chemical Examination'); the two chemists Brackier and Kandel, who, together with Primo Levi, made up 'Die drei Leute vom Labor'. 'Glucksmann, Eugenio' (more correctly Glücksmann) is 'Sergeant Steinlauf' of the 'Initiation' chapter; while 'Alfred Rosenfeld' corresponds to 'Alfred L.' in the chapter 'The Drowned and the Saved'. Finally, there is also Endre Szántó, who is Bandi from the story 'A Disciple' in the collection *Lilìt* [Moments of Reprieve] (1981).

About 800 prisoners who were ill or not in a fit state for the march were abandoned in the camp hospital, among them perhaps 20 Italians (the undersigned was among this number).

The healthy, about 10,000 in number, were made to set out on foot for Gleiwitz, very poorly nourished and equipped. Among the healthy who set out on foot for Gleiwitz were the following individuals:

ABENAIM from Tuscany   he was skilled as a watchmaker
ASSUM from Milan born between 1925 and 1930
BARUCH from Leghorn, born in Smyrna about 25 years old
CARMI CESARE from Genoa
DALLA VOLTA ALBERTO from Brescia, about 24 years old
HALPERN from Zagreb about 25 years old
MANDEL HINKO brother-in-law of the above from Zagreb
SACERDOTI FRANCO from Turin
GLUCKSMANN EUGENIO from Milan
ISRAEL LIKO from Zagreb
ORVIETO from Florence, rabbi, about 25 years old
LEVI Sergio son of Alessandro, from Turin
LEVI ALDO Engineer from Milan
LEVI ALDO Accountant from Milan
LEVI MARIO shopkeeper about 26 years old from Milan
ZELIKOWIC from Zagreb tailor
KLAUSNER ISIDOR Dutch registration no. 169xxx student
   of physics (his wife lived in Zurich) born about 1920
ROSENFELD ALFRED born in Romania, resident of Lor-
   raine, chemical engineer formerly manager of refrigeration
   plants about 42 years old
SILBERLUST ARNOLD about 24 years old student of math-
   ematics, born in Poland, formerly resident in Leipzig
KAMPLAN deported from Borgo S. Dalmazzo, born in the
   Baltic states, formerly a shopkeeper in Milan
KANDEL JEAN about 40 years old, born in Romania, formerly resident in Paris (he had a wife in France) chemist
KAUFMANN GJURI from Nagykanizsa (Hungary) about 26
   years old, chemist
SZANTO ANDREJ (BANDI) Slovakian, studied and graduated in Prague, pharmacist about 30 years old, previously
   deported by the Germans to Ukraine for labour service

SCHLESENGER born about 1919 in Yugoslavia

BRACKIER PALPTIL born in White Russia, Belgian citizen, registration no. 175(884?) resident of Liège? chemist about 35 years old

JEAN SAMUEL from Strasbourg born about 1921 doctor of mathematics

KOSMANN ALFRED from Metz ex Reuter's correspondent in Clairmont Ferrant [*sic* for Clermont-Ferrand]

GRUSZDAS doctor from Alexandria, born in Riga (Latvia) no. 174001 set out on the march in good condition

HIRSCH ERIK born about 1921 very tall

BARABAS SILVIO from Sarajevo, chemist born about 1921 lived in Italy

On the fate of the column dragged off by the retreating Germans, the undersigned has received the following accounts:

[I –]Account of Signor <u>Joe Saltiel</u> from Marseilles (confirmed by Signor Erich Schlochoff from Turin). The column walked for 24 consecutive hours as far as Gleiwitz; a large number of prisoners who got left behind were killed by the guards along the way. The following morning several trains were dispatched from Gleiwitz station, crowded with prisoners (eighty per goods wagon). The train in which Saltiel found himself was halted after 20 kilometres and the prisoners were made to get out in a forest and machine-gunned. Saltiel estimates that the number of those who escaped was very small. He does not know the total number of prisoners on his train and affirms that some Polish peasants compassionately noted down the registration numbers of the corpses.

II – The account of a Dr. Eugenio ? known as Geneg, Polish Christian, concurs with the previous report. Geneg managed to play dead in the forest, and thus escaped the subsequent hunt by the SS for possible survivors to finish off.

III – Enzo Levy from Turin: After the march on foot to Gleiwitz the column, which Levy estimates amounted to at least 18,000 prisoners, became split up in some way that is not entirely clear. Levy found himself in a convoy of goods wagons that was machine-gunned repeatedly. The group of which Levy found himself a member travelled through

Bohemia for several days, halting now and then in deserted Lagers.

During the entire journey a great number of prisoners no longer able to walk were killed and left on the spot.

Levy remembers having passed through Flossemburg [*sic* for Flossenbürg].

IV – From a letter sent to the undersigned by Signor Charles Conreau, French ex-political prisoner, Christian, it appears that none of Signor Conreau's colleagues (of whom several hundred had been deported from the Vosges region to Dachau and from there to Auschwitz in the winter of 1944) had returned to France by September 1945.

V – Hinko Mandel from Zagreb tells of roughly similar events. He was loaded onto a convoy which travelled almost as far as Berlin without being machine-gunned. However, he states that an undetermined but large number of prisoners died during the journey from cold and starvation. He does not recall seeing any Italian prisoners with him.

VI – An Italian civilian worker from Brescia, repatriated a few months ago, has recounted that he found himself with Alberto Della [*sic* for Dalla] Volta from Brescia on the 20 or 21 January in a Lager about 90 Km. away from Auschwitz and already occupied and run by the Russians (Della [*sic*] Volta was deported from Auschwitz along with the transport of 17 January). The worker returned to Italy early and through his own efforts and reports that Della [*sic*] Volta, in a good state of health, intended to stay on in that region to look for his father, who had previously disappeared.

While awaiting other possible depositions, one can suppose for now that a not inconsiderable number of internees of Auschwitz and neighbouring lagers may have escaped extermination. Some of these may still be in the hands of the Russians or the Yugoslavs, or patients in hospitals, and therefore unable to send news of themselves to Italy.

3

Deposition

Primo Levi

[*circa* 1946]

Dr PRIMO LEVI
son of the late Cesare and of Ester Luzzati
born in Turin (Italy) 31 July 1919
resident of Turin, Corso Re Umberto 75

I stayed in the Monowitz Lager (Auschwitz) from 26 February 1944 to 27 January 1945 as a Häftling (registration number 174517).

During this period, I had no way of learning the names of the administrators of the Camp and of those responsible for the inhuman treatment which was reserved for us. Nevertheless, I believe that the responsibility falls collectively on all the

---

Two typed pages with a handwritten signature, drawn up by Levi at the request of the Comitato Ricerche Deportati Ebrei (Search Committee for Jewish Deportees – CRDE) of Rome shortly after his return to Italy. The document was used by Colonel Massimo Adolfo Vitale, the president of the CRDE, who in February 1947 was appointed by the Unione delle Comunità Israelitiche Italiane (Union of Italian Israelite Communities – UCII) and the Ministry of Justice of the Italian Republic to attend the trial in Warsaw of Rudolf Höss, Oberscharführer (Commandant) of the Auschwitz-Birkenau Lager.

soldiers, petty officers and officers of the Waffen-SS in charge of our camp, and in particular on the general and medical management of the Lager.

As is now well known, only about one-fifth of each convoy of deportees was admitted to the camp on their arrival, namely those who, at first sight, were considered fit for manual labour. All the others (the elderly, the children, the sick and most of the women) were immediately sent to the asphyxiation chambers, and their bodies cremated.

All those who were forcibly admitted to the camp were stripped completely naked and deprived without exception of all their personal possessions. The internal statistics of the camp demonstrate that only in exceptional cases was it possible to survive in the Lager for more than three or four months. Insufficient food, lack of suitable clothing, extremely hard labour and beatings soon got the better of even the strongest constitution.

The SS periodically carried out inspections in the camp to look for the chronically sick and those unfit for work ('Selections'). These too were sent in their turn, and completely aware of their fate, to the asphyxiation chambers and the crematory.

Any attempt at escape, and any even minor disciplinary offence, was punished by hanging. For these reasons, no more than 2% of the Italians in the Monowitz (Auschwitz) camp were able to return to their country.

As a result of my personal researches, naturally carried out after the liberation, I am able to affirm that even in their choice of the method of elimination the executioners of the Auschwitz central command displayed a deliberate and inconceivable ferocity. The poison used by them in the gas chambers consisted of a product called 'Zyklon B'. This substance was not intended for such a purpose; it was manufactured as a pesticide and disinfectant, in particular to rid ships' holds and warehouses of rats. It was made from prussic acid with the addition of irritants and lachrymatory substances to make its presence more detectable in case of leaks or breakages of the receptacles in which it was contained. Consequently, it can be assumed that the agony of the unfortunates condemned to death must have been unbelievably painful.

Gold teeth were extracted from the corpses of those eliminated and their hair was cut off and stored separately for
some as yet unknown purpose. The ashes from their bodies
were used as agricultural fertilizer.

In witness whereof

                                        Primo Levi

4

Deposition on Monowitz

Leonardo De Benedetti

[1946?]

On 27 August 1945 there appeared before us, Colonel Vitale Massimo Adolfo, son of the late Giuseppe, President of the Comitato Richerche Deportati Ebrei [Search Committee for Jewish Deportees], at the headquarters of the said Committee, Lungo Tevere Sanzio 9, Rome – Dr. LEONARDO DE BENEDETTI – holder of Identity Card No. 520790 – who gave the following deposition concerning his period of detention in the German concentration camps from February 1944 to January 1945:

At the beginning of December 1943, I tried to cross into Switzerland with my wife and some other people, but when we reached Lanzo di Intelvi we were immediately spotted and arrested by a border guard patrol who took us to their barracks, from where after a few days we were transferred, with a military police escort, to Modena Prison and from there, on 21 December 1943, to the camp at Fossoli. We left this camp on 22 February 1944 and after about eight days we reached Auschwitz.

Editors' title. The text (three typed pages with a typed signature) is preserved in Milan in the Archive of the CDEC, Centro di Documentazione Ebraica Contemporanea (Centre for Contemporary Jewish Research). The deposition was probably transcribed by Colonel Vitale. The date of 27 August 1945 is certainly incorrect as this was prior to Leonardo De Benedetti's return to Italy.

On the same evening that we arrived, my wife Iolanda together with 300 other women and several hundred men were sent to the gas chamber.

During the period of quarantine I was tattooed with the number 174489 and sent to the Monowitz camp where I remained for exactly eleven months, up until the liberation carried out by the Russians on 26 January 1945.

I do not remember the names of the camp commandants apart from that of Dr. MENGELE – the medical captain of the SS who carried out the final examination of the unfortunates destined for the gas chambers. It was he, indeed, who ruled me out no fewer than four times because I told him, as I passed in front of him, that I was a doctor. But I do not believe that I owe my life to his spirit of professional solidarity but rather to the fact that orders were to spare the lives of doctors who found themselves deported to the camp.

Monowitz was one of 100 'Lagers' under the authority of the Central Administration of Auschwitz where, as in all the other camps, the most dreadful atrocities and iniquities were committed continually and as a matter of course, owing to the regulations governing the general administration of the Lagers.

The Monowitz camp was not a 'Vernichtungslager', that is to say one of those camps where deportees were housed for a few days, at the end of which they were brutally slaughtered, either by mass shootings or by gas; it was an 'Arbeitslager', which is to say a forced labour camp, in which the destruction of the Jews was entrusted to the impossible living conditions, to lack of food, superhuman toil, insufficient protection against bad weather and the harshness of the seasons, and in addition those who did not die from disease but reached such a state of physical exhaustion that they were unable to carry out forced labour would be eliminated in the gas chambers. Lastly, others accused of infringements of the disciplinary regulations of the camp would be hanged, a monstrous punishment out of all proportion to the offence, which was utterly negligible or even non-existent. Who, for instance, would consider it a 'crime' for a prisoner to try to escape. And yet a considerable number of unfortunates were publicly hanged in front of all the other deportees for that very reason!!!!

We lived foully crowded together in the most nauseating filth, with no possibility of taking care of our personal hygiene, defencelessly exposed to the likelihood of contagions, infections and infestations; we were deprived from our arrival of all our own clothes and were poorly dressed, like convicts, in garments of striped cloth which constituted a derisory barrier against the cold, the damp, the rain and the snow. Inadequately fed on two rations a day of soup made from turnips and cabbage leaves plus a meagre amount of bread, a bread made from various ingredients, of which the greatest number were those least digestible and nourishing.

Moreover, we were forced, from the very first days of our arrival in the camp, and without even a reasonable period of training, to carry out various forms of labour for which none of us had sufficient aptitude or the necessary physical qualifications.

The living conditions were just as insupportable from a psychological and moral point of view, since the orders of those in command were directed, before eliminating a man, at eliminating his personality, starting with his name which, as is well known, was replaced by a number tattooed on to the skin of the left forearm. No psychological or cultural human value was taken into account, but everyone without distinction became part of an amorphous mass kept under control by fear and by corporal punishment. In a few days, every deportee was reduced to the level of an animal for whom the only reason for living was a ration of bread or a mess-tin of soup.

It is easy to understand why a good many individuals fell prey, a few days after their arrival, to the most profound depression and preferred an immediate and voluntary death to a delayed one after a succession of suffering and acts of violence, and so deliberately approached the barbed wire, through which there ran a high-voltage current, in order to be electrocuted by it.

Having driven a number of people into such a mental state is no less of a crime than to have murdered them with one's own hands.

Up until the end of 1943, the deportees, whatever their physical condition, even if they were seriously ill, were forced to work without receiving treatment of any kind.

After that date, the beginnings of a medical service were set up, to which doctors deported to the camp were assigned, under the direction of German doctors. Passing a cursory medical examination would give a few days' rest to those who were temporarily unfit; for those more seriously ill, and therefore not recoverable for work, the infirmary was the waiting-room for the gas chamber. It was there that the selections mainly took place, in which the most debilitated prisoners were singled out, or those whose state of health was such that they could no longer be employed as labourers. These unfortunates would be sent to the gas chambers, and along with them the tuberculous, the malarial and the syphilitic, even if clinically cured and only found out through their own unwary and ingenuous confession. The organization of the infirmary was completely unsatisfactory from a sanitary point of view; the premises too small in relation to the number of patients; these, devoid of any kind of bedlinen, lay completely naked, two by two on a single pallet, with a pair of ragged and threadbare blankets, horribly soiled with the most disgusting stains. In an isolation block lay, haphazardly crowded together, patients suffering from the most contagious diseases: typhus, diphtheria, measles, scarlet fever, erysipelas, etc. – infections always present in the camp in an endemic form. That block housed those unfortunates for a few days or a very few hours before they were dispatched to their death in the gas chambers.

Drugs were almost entirely lacking, and the few existing ones were given out with such parsimony as to render their employment more or less useless. Practically speaking, the sick were abandoned to themselves, and for most of those who got out, their lot was no better, since the exit from the infirmary represented the entrance to the gas chambers.

To these were also sent, I do not know on the basis of what criteria, a certain number of prisoners as soon as they arrived. The passengers of the convoys which transported deportees from all over Europe would be divided as soon as they got off the trains into two columns, one of which, the less numerous, would be sent to one of the various concentration camps, while the other would be taken away for immediate extermination.

Torino 3/3/1947

Spett. COMITATO RICERCHE DEPORTATI EBREI
Roma

_____

Facendo riscontro a Vs. pregiata del 28
u.s., mi affretto ad aderire alla Vostra richiesta, riassumendo in
appresso quanto ai personale e specifico potrei esporre davanti al
Tribunale di Varsavia.

1) Ho assistito personalmente al seguente episodio: Dopo che il
mio Lager (Monowitz, presso Auschwitz) fu abbandonato dalla guarnigione
gione di SS, fuggiti in extremis davanti all'avanzata russa, 18 prigionieri si stabilirono entro la casermetta abbandonata, per atten-
dervi i liberatori. Pochi giorni dopo passò per caso accanto al campo un gruppo di SS dispersi, essi pure in fuga; essi, dopo un somma-
rio esame dei campo, uccisero senz'altro i 18 prigionieri, con colpi
di revolver a bruciapelo, e ne allineronoi cadaveri lungo la strada.
Essi non avevano evidentemente ricevuto ordini in tal senso, ed agiva-
no di loro iniziativa. Potrei riconoscere i loro visi.

II) Come già ho accennato nel mio 1° rapporto, il veleno usato nelle camere a gas di Auschwitz, e da me esaminato, non era stato creato
dall'industria tedesca per questo uso specifico. Esso conteneva, oltre al principio tossico, una sostanza corrosiva ed irritante per le
mucose, che doveva quindi rendere atrocemente penosi gli ultimi minuti
delle vittime.

III) Il lavoro prestato dai prigionieri del mio campo si svolgeva
nella fabbrica di Buna-Monowitz, a 7 km. da Auschwitz, sotto la direzione del nominato Doctor Ingenieur PANNWITZ, ingegnere chimico della
I.G. Farbenindustrie. Ignoro se costui figuri fra gli imputati, ma lo
ritengo comunque colpevole, per essersi sempre mostrato di estrema du-
rezza ed esigenza, sovraccaricando i prigionieri di lavoro oltre ogni
limite ragionevole, e denunziando alle SS senza pietà ogni più piccola
mancanza.

IV) Fra il personale addetto al campo in senso stretto, ricordo
nome e fisionomia del Dott. MENGELE, sovraintendente sanitario di tutti i campi del gruppo Auschwitz. Potrei inoltre riconoscere facilmente
le figure di due fra i diretti responsabili di tutte le quotidiane
sevizie ed iniquità del mio campo: il Lagerälteste, delinquente pro-
fessionale tedesco, nativo di Breslavia, ed il Lagerkapo, sedicente
politico, egli pure tedesco. Dal primo fui io stesso percosso più volte fino al sangue. Di entrambi ignoro i nomi.

Mi permetto infine di aggiungere alcune note personali: sono lau-
reato in Chimica; ho lavorato a Monowitz-Auschwitz dal febbraio '44 al
gennaio '45; non ho mai ricoperto cariche in Lager, nè comunque colla-
borato colla Direzione del campo. Parlo il francese, l'inglese e il
tedesco. Sono già in possesso di regolare Passaporto.
Allego la richiesta Dichiarazione di residenza. Con perfetta
osservanza

Dott. Primo Levi

Dott. Primo LEVI- c-Re Umberto 75- TORINO
tel.660.025

Figure 5 Primo Levi, 'Statement for the Höss Trial' (Archive of the
Centre for Contemporary Jewish Research (CDEC), Milan, Fondo
Massimo Adolfo Vitale, b. 3, fasc. 115).

5

Statement for the Höss Trial

Primo Levi

[1947]

Turin, 3 March 1947

Comitato ricerche deportati ebrei [Search Committee for Jewish Deportees], Rome

Dear Sirs,
In reply to your letter of the 28 inst., I hasten to comply with your request, summarizing below what I would be able to attest to in the way of personal and specific evidence before the Warsaw Tribunal.

I) I personally witnessed the following incident: after my Lager (Monowitz, near Auschwitz) was abandoned by the SS garrison, fleeing in extremis before the Russian

---

Editors' title. Typed letter with handwritten signature, preserved in Milan in the CDEC Archive. Levi was replying to a request from Colonel Vitale concerning the specific contribution which he would be able to make to the Höss trial. Levi wished to attach to this statement a typed copy of 'The Story of Ten Days', which he had just finished writing and which would become the final chapter of his first book, *If This is a Man*.

advance, eighteen prisoners moved into the deserted barracks to wait for the liberators there. A few days later, it so happened that a disbanded group of SS passed by the camp, themselves also fleeing; and after a perfunctory inspection of the camp they indubitably killed the eighteen prisoners with revolver shots at point blank range, and lined their corpses up along the road. They had clearly not received orders to do so, and acted on their own initiative. I would be able to recognize their faces.

II) As I have already mentioned in my 1st report, the poison used in the Auschwitz gas chambers, as investigated by me, was not produced by German industry for that specific purpose. It contained, in addition to the toxic principle, a corrosive substance, irritating to the mucous membranes, which must therefore have made the final minutes of the victims agonizingly painful.

III) The labour performed by the prisoners in my camp was carried out in the Buna-Monowitz factory, 7 km from Auschwitz, under the direction of the aforenamed Doctor Engineer PANNWITZ, the chemical engineer of I.G. Farbenindustrie. I do not know whether he is listed among the accused, but I consider him to be guilty in any case for the extreme harshness and exigency he always displayed, overloading the prisoners with work beyond any reasonable limit and pitilessly denouncing to the SS any shortcoming, however slight.

IV) Among the personnel in charge of the camp in the strict sense, I remember the name and face of Dr MENGELE, the medical superintendent of all the camps in the Auschwitz group. I would also easily be able to recognize the appearance of two of those directly responsible for all the everyday running and the iniquities of my camp: the *Lagerälteste*, a German professional criminal, a native of Breslau, and the *Lagerkapo*, a self-styled politician, also a German. The first of these many times beat me till I bled. I do not know either of their names.

Finally, permit me to add a few personal details: I have a degree in Chemistry; I worked in Monowitz-Auschwitz from

February '44 to January '45; I never held any official post in the Lager, and nor did I collaborate in any way with the Administration of the camp. I speak French, English and German. I already hold a valid Passport.

I enclose the requested Declaration of residence. Yours respectfully,

Dr Primo Levi

6

Deposition for the Höss Trial

Leonardo De Benedetti

[1947]

Although my stay in the Monowitz Concentration Camp – one of the hundred 'Lagers' under the authority of the Central Administration of Auschwitz – lasted for exactly eleven months (from 26 February 1944 to 26 January 1945), I am not able to point to particular acts in connection with the aforenamed Hoess, but can only recall and denounce the generic atrocities and iniquities of which I was the witness and many times the victim, without being able to specify whether these were due, as is very likely, to the precise regulations of the General Administration of the 'Lager' or to the personal initiative of the Commandant of the Monowitz camp. But since everything abominable, evil, violent, savage and contrary to the most elementary laws of humanity to which the prisoners of the Monowitz Camp were subjected was exactly paralleled by what took place in the other ninety-nine camps

---

Editors' title. The text is preserved in the Biblioteca 'Emanuele Artom' della Comunità Ebraica di Torino (Emanuele Artom Library of the Jewish Community of Turin). The deposition was written for the Höss trial, which opened in Warsaw on 11 March 1947. Leonardo De Benedetti went there in person to give evidence. On 2 April, the sentence of death by hanging was pronounced, carried out on 16 April on the Appellplatz of the Auschwitz Lager where Höss had exercised his power.

under the Auschwitz Administration, it is a very easy and obvious deduction that all this was planned and carried out according to definite orders issued by a single central body.

The Monowitz Camp was not, theoretically, a 'Vernichtungslager', that is to say one of those Camps where Deportees were housed for a few days, at the end of which they were brutally slaughtered, either by mass shootings or by gas; it was an 'Arbeitslager', which is to say a forced labour camp, in which nevertheless the pre-ordained destruction of the Jews was entrusted to the impossible living conditions, to lack of food, superhuman toil, insufficient protection against bad weather and the harshness of the seasons; in addition, those who did not die from disease but reached such a state of physical exhaustion that they were unable to carry out forced labour would be eliminated in the gas chambers. Lastly, others, accused of infringements of the disciplinary regulations of the Camp, would be hanged, a punishment monstrously out of proportion to the offence which, according to the strictures of reason and the spirit of humanity, was utterly negligible or even non-existent. Who, for instance, would consider it a 'crime' for a prisoner to try to escape?

I have described the living conditions imposed on the prisoners as 'impossible': 'impossible' not only from the physical perspective, as they lived crowded foully together in the most nauseating filth, with no possibility of taking care of their personal hygiene, defencelessly exposed to the likelihood of contagions, infections and infestations; deprived from their arrival of all their own clothes, the prisoners were poorly dressed in the striped garments of convicts, which constituted a derisory barrier against the cold, the damp, the rain and the snow; inadequately fed on two rations a day of soup made from turnips and cabbage leaves plus a meagre amount of bread, a bread made from various ingredients of which the greatest number were those least digestible and nourishing, the deportees were forced, from the very first days of their arrival in the Camp, and without even a reasonable period of training, to carry out manual labour for which, one may say, none of them had either sufficient aptitude or the necessary physical qualifications. But those living conditions were just as impossible from a psychological and moral point of view, since the organization of the camp was directed, before eliminating a man, to eliminating his personality, starting with his name which, as is well known, was replaced by a number tattooed on to the skin of the left forearm; no psychological or cultural human value was taken into account, but everyone without distinction became part of an amorphous mass kept under control by fear and by corporal punishment; in a few days, every prisoner was reduced to the level of an animal for whom the only reason for living was a ration of bread and a mess-tin of soup. Under these conditions, perhaps the major mental activity of each deportee was directed towards finding a more or less legitimate way of getting hold of some extra bread or soup and of evading the surveillance of the work squad overseers for a few minutes in order to rest a little.

It is very understandable that a good many individuals fell prey, a few days after their arrival, to the most profound depression and preferred an immediate, voluntary death to a delayed one after a succession of suffering and enduring acts of violence, and so deliberately approached the barbed wire, through which there ran a high-voltage current, in order to be electrocuted by it; having driven a number of people into such a mental state is no less of a crime than to have murdered them with one's own hands.

There was an infirmary inside the Camp, which was set up towards the end of 1943; before that time, the camp was completely without a medical service of any kind and the prisoners not only had no possibility of being treated if they were ill, but were forced to continue with their usual labour just the same, whatever their physical condition. It was indeed at the end of 1943 that the beginnings of a medical service were set up, perhaps more through the initiative of some interned doctors anxious to be assigned to work which fitted their skills and professional training than through the good offices of the Camp Administration; subsequently, around this medical service, consisting of a Clinic where patients would present themselves to undergo a cursory examination and obtain a few days' rest if deemed to be temporarily unfit, there grew up a bona fide Infirmary which, though it did indeed provide treatment after a fashion to patients who were less seriously ill and therefore recoverable for work, represented for most of the invalids nothing but the waiting-room for the gas chamber. In fact, it was in the Infirmary that the so-called 'selections' mainly took place, in which the most debilitated prisoners were singled out, whose state of health was such that they could no longer be employed as labourers. These would be sent to the 'gas chambers', and along with them the tuberculous, the malarial and the syphilitic, the last two even if clinically cured and only found out through their own unwary and ingenuous confession.

The organization of the Infirmary was completely unsatisfactory from a sanitary point of view; premises too small in relation to the number of patients; these, devoid of any kind of bed-linen, lay completely naked, two by two on a single pallet, with a pair of ragged and threadbare blankets, horribly soiled with the most disgusting stains. In an isolation block lay, haphazardly crowded together, patients suffering from the most contagious diseases: typhus, diphtheria, measles, scarlet fever, erysipelas, etc. – infections always present in the camp in an endemic state.

It is perhaps needless to mention that the most indispensible drugs were largely missing, while the rest were in such short supply that they were distributed with a parsimony which rendered their employment more or less useless. Practically speaking, the patients were abandoned to themselves, and for most of those who got out, it was not to a better fate, since the exit from the infirmary represented the entrance to the gas chambers.

To these were also sent, it is not known on the basis of what criteria, a certain number of prisoners as soon as they arrived; the passengers of the convoys which transported deportees from all over Europe would be divided as soon as they got off the trains into two columns, one of which, the less numerous, would be sent to one of the various concentration Camps, while the other would be made to get into trucks and would be taken away for immediate extermination.

7

Testimony for a Fellow Prisoner

Primo Levi

[1953]

Vanda Maestro, in contact from 25 July 1943 with members of the Partito d'Azione [Action Party], found herself in the December of that year in the Val d'Aosta as a member of a newly formed Partisan band, with various assignments (making contacts down in the valley, distributing leaflets, occasional exploratory missions to discover the movements of German and Fascist troops). She was 24 years old, and had recently graduated from university.

Published with the author's name unspecified in the volume *Donne piemontesi nella lotta di liberazione: 99 partigiane cadute, 185 deportate, 38 cadute civili* [Piedmontese Women in the Struggle for Liberation: 99 Fallen Partisans, 185 Deported, 38 Civilian Dead] edited by the Women's Branch of the ANPI (Associazione Nazionale Partigiani d'Italia; National Association of Italian Partisans) of Turin, without a date but printed in December 1953.

Given the anonymous form of the text, it is useful to mention that Vanda Maestro was arrested at Amay, in the Valle d'Aosta, with Primo Levi and Luciana Nissim, in the course of a search carried out by military units of the Republic of Salò, Benito Mussolini's puppet government which, under the control of the Nazis, at that time dominated the north and centre of the Italian peninsula. Together with her two friends, Vanda was transferred to the Fossoli-Carpi concentration camp and from there she was deported to Auschwitz with them in the same sealed wagon.

Anyone who saw her then, on those tracks already buried under the snow, cannot forget her delicate little face, marked by physical exertion and by a more profound tension, since, for her, as for the best of those in that situation at that time, the choice had not been easy, nor happy, nor problem-free.

Orphaned at a young age by the death of her mother, Vanda was governed and often overwhelmed by an extremely acute sensitivity, which allowed her to read the innermost thoughts of those around her. Her mind was sincere and direct and she was unaware, or else disdainful, of all those stratagems, those smoke-screens, those intentional oversights and illusions with which we protect ourselves as best we can against the onslaughts of the world. Therefore, no one was more exposed to suffering than she was, and her capacity for suffering was almost limitless. One perceived in her a depth of constant sorrow, conscious and accepted and resolutely unspoken, which gained her everyone's immediate respect.

She was not by nature a strong woman: she was afraid of death, and more even than death she feared physical pain. The strength she displayed in those days matured little by little; it was the fruit of a resolution renewed minute by minute.

But her partisan experience was brief. On 13 December, she was caught in a round-up intended to capture a more important band which operated in an adjoining valley. She was arrested, taken to Aosta, interrogated at length. She answered cleverly, in such a way that she could not be charged with anything concrete regarding her activities, but since she was Jewish she was sent to Fossoli, and from there to a Lager with a now infamous name: to the women's camp of Birkenau-Auschwitz.

Here, for this gentle, loyal, generous little woman, there must have unfolded with appalling slowness, month after month, the most hideous of fates that a man in a paroxysm of hatred could imagine and wish on his own worst enemies. Those who returned from Birkenau have told us about Vanda, worn down from the first few days by exhaustion and hardship and by that terrible clear-sightedness of hers which forced her to reject the merciful delusions to which we surrender so willingly when faced with the ultimate threat. They have described to us her poor head shorn of its hair, her limbs soon wasted by disease and starvation, all the stages of that nefarious process of crushing and extinguishing which in the Lager was the prelude to physical death.

And we know everything, or almost everything, about her end: her name pronounced among those of the condemned, her descent from the bunk in the infirmary, her setting off (in full consciousness!) towards the gas chamber and the cremation oven.

8

Anniversary

Primo Levi

[1955]

Ten years on from the liberation of the Lagers, it is sad
and significant to have to observe that, in Italy at any rate,
the subject of the extermination camps, far from becoming
history, is heading towards total oblivion.

It is unnecessary, here, to recall the figures; to recall that
this was the most enormous massacre in history, such as to
reduce practically to zero, for example, the Jewish population
of entire countries in eastern Europe; to recall that, if Nazi
Germany had been able to carry out her plan to its conclusion, the technology tested out at Auschwitz and elsewhere
would have been applied, with the well-known thoroughness
of the Germans, to entire continents.

Nowadays, it is indelicate to talk about the Lagers. One
risks being accused, at best, of having a persecution complex
or a gratuitous love of the macabre; at worst, of pure and
simple mendacity, or even of offending against decency.

Is this silence justified? Must we tolerate it, we survivors?
Must they tolerate it who, petrified with fear and revulsion, witnessed, among blows, curses and savage yells, the

Published in *Torino* [Turin], 31 (4 April 1955), special issue for the
tenth anniversary of the Liberation from the Nazi–Fascist occupation (25 April 1945).

departure of the sealed wagons; and, years later, the return of the very few survivors, broken in body and spirit? Is it right to regard it as expended, that task of bearing witness which once was felt to be a necessity and an urgent duty?

There can be only one reply. It is not permissible to forget, it is not permissible to keep silent. If we keep silent, who will speak? Certainly not the culprits and their accomplices. If our testimony is missing, in a not-too-distant future the tales of Nazi brutality, due to their very enormity, could be relegated to the realm of legends. So, speak we must.

Yet the silence prevails. There is a silence that is the result of an uneasy conscience, or indeed of a bad conscience; it is the silence of those who, when invited or compelled to pass judgement, attempt in any way they can to deflect the discussion, bringing up nuclear weapons, carpet bombing, the Nuremberg trials and the issue of the Soviet labour camps: subjects not without weight in themselves, but completely without significance as any kind of moral justification for the Fascist crimes which, by their nature and extent, constitute a monument of such ferocity that its equal cannot be found in the entire history of humanity.

But it will not be out of place to mention another aspect of this silence, this reticence, this evasion. That they should keep silent about this in Germany, that the Fascists should keep silent, is natural and, all things considered, not unwelcome to us. Their words would be of no use to us; we have no time for their ludicrous attempts to justify themselves. But what shall we say about the silence of the civilized world, about the silence of culture, about our own silence in front of our children, in front of friends returning from long years of exile in far-off lands? It is not due simply to weariness, to the attrition of the years, to the normal attitude of 'primum vivere'. It is not due to cowardice. There lives within us a more profound and more worthy impulse which in many circumstances urges us to keep silent about the Lagers, or at least to minimize and censor the images of them, still so vivid in our memory.

It is shame. We are men, we belong to the same human family to which our torturers belonged. Confronted by the enormity of their guilt, we feel that we too are citizens of Sodom and Gomorrah; we are not able to feel exempt from the accusation which an extra-terrestrial judge, on the basis of our own testimony, would level against the whole of humankind.

We are the children of the Europe where Auschwitz exists; we live in the century in which science was warped and gave birth to the racial laws and the gas chambers. Who can safely say that he is immune from infection?

And still more remains to be said: painful and bitter things which will not sound unfamiliar to anyone who has read *Les armes de la nuit*. It is futile to call the death of the countless victims of the extermination camps a glorious one. It was not glorious: it was a defenceless and naked, ignominious and filthy death. Nor is slavery honourable; there were those who were able to undergo it unscathed, exceptions to be regarded with respectful wonder, but it is an essentially ignoble condition, the source of almost irresistible debasement and moral shipwreck.

It is right that these things should be said, because they are true. But let it be clear that this does not mean lumping together victims and murderers; this does not lessen the guilt of the Fascists and Nazis but, on the contrary, makes it a hundred times worse. They demonstrated for all the centuries to come what unsuspected reserves of ferocity and madness lie dormant in man after thousands of years of civilized life, and this is demonic work. They laboured tenaciously to create their monstrous machine, the generator of death and corruption; a greater crime would be impossible to imagine. They insolently constructed their realm with the tools of hatred, violence and lies; their downfall is a warning.

9

Denunciation against
Dr Joseph Mengele

Leonardo De Benedetti

[*circa* 1959]

The Undersigned, Dr Leonardo DE-BENEDETTI, born in
Turin on 15 September 1898 and residing there at 61 Corso
Re Umberto, physician and surgeon by profession, at the
request of the International Auschwitz Committee, which
intends to lodge my denunciation with the Public Prosecutor's
office of the court of Freiburg im Breisgau to facilitate the
legal process which it has instituted in order to obtain the
extradition from Argentina of the ex-SS Hauptsturmführer
Dr Joseph MENGELE, formerly doctor of the Auschwitz
camp, I declare as follows:

I was deported from Italy, on account of being a Jew, on
20 February 1944 and arrived at Auschwitz station on the

Five typed pages with a handwritten signature, preserved in the
Biblioteca 'Emanuele Artom' della Comunità Ebraica di Torino
(Emanuele Artom Library of the Jewish Community of Turin).
In 1959, the International Auschwitz Committee, based in
Vienna, filed a complaint against Josef Mengele with the State Pros-
ecutor in Freiburg im Breisgau, the most recent place of residence
of the Auschwitz doctor, whose last traces were left there in 1954.
On 5 June 1959, the Prosecutor issued an arrest warrant, while
the West German Foreign Office made an extradition request to
Argentina. De Benedetti produced this statement at a date relatively
close to these initiatives.

evening of 26 February 1944. The convoy of which I was a part consisted of 650 people, of whom the oldest was aged 85 and the youngest 6 months. As soon as we got off the train, the first selection took place right there on the station platform; I had the good fortune to be judged young enough and still fit for work, while my wife (who was with me and from whom I was suddenly and brutally separated) was sent that same night to the Gas Chamber, as I learnt, after the liberation, from some of her companions who survived. The same evening I, with another 95 companions, was transported straight to the MONOWITZ-BUNA Camp, where I received the Registration No. 174489 and where I remained until 17 January 1945, when I was liberated by the Red Army. During the whole eleven months I had to work as a labourer in various 'Kommandos', all very demanding; the work always involved unloading or carrying. Having never succeeded in getting the 'Arbeitsdienst' to recognize that I was a doctor, I was not given the chance to enter the 'Krankenbau' as a doctor, or even just as a nurse.

My physical condition naturally underwent a rapid and serious collapse due to the extremely hard labour to which I – like all the other prisoners – was subjected and which it is not necessary to describe here, also because by now the conditions of life in the Lagers are well known to everyone. Just as it is known to everyone that every so often the so-called 'Selections' would take place in the Lagers – which is to say, the examination of the physical condition of the prisoners to check their capacity for work; those who, as a consequence of exhaustion, physical abuse, starvation or disease, were reduced to such a debilitated state as to compromise their ability to withstand the punishing labour would be sent to the Gas Chambers.

These selections, in the Monowitz Camp, took place in two stages: the preliminary decision was made by an SS officer, attended by the doctors of the Camp Krankenbau, and a few days later Dr Mengele would arrive to ratify, by means of a second examination, just as quick and superficial, the decision originally made. Both these examinations were, as I have said, absurdly perfunctory: a glance was enough to make a judgement; and if, after the preliminary decision, there lingered in the most optimistic a hope, however feeble and ingenuous, of still being saved, the second decision – the one made by Dr Mengele – was final, and represented a judgement against which there was no appeal and an irrevocable sentence of death.

Dr Mengele always appeared in the camp in impeccable uniform, elegant almost to the point of refinement, with very shiny high boots, leather gloves, and a riding crop in his hand; and while he carried out the terrible examination he assumed a smiling and almost kindly expression; with his crop, as those he was judging paraded at the double, naked, under his gaze and stopped for a moment in front of him, he indicated with supreme indifference the group to which his infallible judgement had assigned the prisoner: to the left, the condemned; to the right, the very few lucky ones whom he judged still fit for work, at least until the next selection.

At this point I must record my own experience of the selections and how on each of the four occasions when I passed Dr Mengele's examination I managed to save myself from a fatal judgement. For this reason, I need to begin by relating the lucky incident which happened to me on one of the first days after my arrival in the Monowitz camp, when, to my good fortune, I found that a work mate in the Kommando to which I had been assigned was a colleague, already a camp elder, who informed me about the life of the camp, with all the regulations, prohibitions and dangers to which its operations were subject; he was a doctor from Alsace, I think from Strasbourg, a certain Dr Klotz, whom sadly I lost sight of a little while later and never had the chance to meet again – nor did I ever hear anything more of him, something I greatly regret, not least because I was never able to thank him for his valuable advice, to one piece of which in particular I believe that I owe my life. In fact, among other things, he advised me always to remember in every hostile situation to declare that I was a doctor, and in particular to make this clear if I had been included in a list of prisoners to be transferred, especially if I was being cajoled into thinking I was being sent to a so-called light labour camp. He hinted to me, without wishing to say precisely what it involved, about the danger of these 'transports' and, perhaps in order not to frighten me too much, was unwilling to confirm – although without denying the possibility – the existence of the Gas Chambers about which I had already heard rumours; he simply told me that there were definitely no Gas Chambers at Monowitz; it could well be that there were some elsewhere, although he had never seen them; but in any case it was as well to remain at all costs at Monowitz, which was why the only chance of safety in dangerous circumstances lay in pointing out that one was a doctor.

I did not forget this advice; and every time I had to parade in front of Dr Mengele I had the strength to say in a loud voice, 'Ich bin ein Italiener Arzt'; at which my judge asked me some questions to assure himself of the truth of my claim, then assigned me to the group of the saved.

I do not know whether this concern for doctors was the result of Dr Mengele's personal initiative, or whether in saving his colleagues he was simply obeying orders received from on high; I am really not in a position to support one hypothesis rather than the other, though I think it stands to reason on several counts that the second is the more plausible. That is to say, I do not believe that Dr Mengele, SS Hauptsturmführer, would have been capable of abstracting himself from his SS mind-set and taking account of the particular professional status of a certain group of people in order to pronounce one judgement rather than another; doctors or not, all he saw in front of him were Jews, and as such they had to be eliminated if their physical condition rendered them useless as labourers; and he – SS Hauptsturmführer – could not allow himself to be moved by a trivial coincidence of professional colleague-ship without betraying the fundamental principles of the Nazi theories to which he had sworn unswerving loyalty.

For this reason, it is a great deal more likely that in saving Jewish doctors he was simply following orders received from on high in consideration of the possible utility, in immediate or future circumstances, of those particular individuals.

However, even if this hypothesis was unfounded and on the contrary the former was true, that would in no way reduce the scale of the crime committed by the above-named Dr Joseph Mengele; with this gesture he would have saved the lives of no more than a tiny number of individuals, as against the thousands and thousands of poor wretches that, with a small, indifferent gesture, made with a smile on his lips, he had sent to their deaths.

In my case, there is nothing else that I can lay to the charge of Dr Mengele from first-hand knowledge; I do not know how great a part he played, for example, in organizing so-called scientific research using 'human guinea pigs', nor about his personal part in such research; I know that charges of this kind have also been laid against him, but I have no direct evidence which would enable me to support them with my own testimony. But the part which he took in organizing and causing the extermination of so many people (to which I can bear witness with complete certainty) seems to me to be in itself a crime so monstrous as to justify, with regard to Dr Mengele, the most severe and implacable sentence.

10

Letter to a Fascist's Daughter Who Wants to Know the Truth

Primo Levi

[1959]

A reader writes:

'I am a twelve-year-old middle school pupil, and like many of my classmates I went to see the exhibition about German concentration camps which finishes on Sunday. Afterwards, we all started discussing it, with some feeling doubtful, some saying that the exhibition is just anti-German propaganda, some saying it is exaggerated and some claiming that it is all true.

One of my classmates says that "if those things had really happened, there would be some mention of them in our

---

Editors' title. A public correspondence between Primo Levi and a very young reader of Turin's leading newspaper, *La Stampa*, 29 November and 3 December 1959, in the 'Specchio dei tempi' [Mirror of the Times] column.

On 14 November 1959, a Deportation Exhibition opened in Turin, in the Palazzo Carignano. This exhibition had already been touring for four years, beginning in Carpi (in whose environs, it is important to repeat, the Fossoli concentration camp was set up). The interest generated in Turin by the exhibition prompted the city to organize two evenings of 'Talks for Young People' on 4 and 5 December 1959, which drew 1,300 listeners on the first evening and 1,500 on the second. In his role as a witness, Levi spoke on both evenings, replying to the questions of the audience; in all probability, this was his first public appearance.

history books". Another says: "If those photos were really
genuine, I think they would have been able to enlarge them
and have an exhibition like the one on the family of man at
Palazzo Madama." Others say that they don't want to make
us study the last war precisely because such terrible things
happened. The teachers agree with those who think like that.
They sigh and say, "it's unfortunate", but I want someone to
tell me more about it. I, the daughter of a Fascist, was left
terrified by what I saw and I have prayed to God that my
father is innocent of this massacre.

Also, I want to say to the people who put on exhibitions
that they should arrange them with more space. In order
to see it (and I wasn't able to look closely at many of the
pictures, which were too high up) I had to go no fewer than
three times.

A Fascist's daughter who wants to know the truth'

Primo Levi, the author of *If This is a Man*, a book about
the extermination camps which has now been translated
world-wide, writes:

'On behalf of the Associazione ex-Deportati [Associa-
tion of Ex-Deportees] which organized the Exhibition on
the German concentration camps, I should like to thank the
reader who "wants to know the truth", because her letter,
published in "Mirror of the Times", is the letter we have
been waiting for.

No, signorina, there is no way of doubting the truth of
those images. Those things really happened and they happened like this: not centuries ago, not in distant lands, but
15 years ago, and in the heart of this Europe of ours. Anyone
who doubts this only has to get on a train and visit what is
left of those evil places. And not even that is necessary; here,
in our own city, there are dozens of eye-witnesses; there are
thousands (even women, even children: children!) who ended
up lost in those mounds of bones, and bear witness by their
absence, by the void they have left behind.

We can understand, but we cannot approve of those teachers who "sigh and say *it's unfortunate*". They are human
beings just like us, and just like the authors and the perpetrators of the massacres; it is not strange that many people,

even innocent ones, feel ashamed when faced with these facts and prefer to keep silent. But in this case silence is a mistake, almost a crime; the very (unexpected) success of the exhibition confirms this. There is a hunger for the truth, in spite of everything; therefore, we must not conceal the truth. The shame and the silence of the innocent can mask the guilty silence of the perpetrators, allowing them to defer and evade the judgement of history.

I too hope that the reader's father is innocent, and it is very likely that he is since things happened differently in Italy. But the exhibition is addressed not to fathers but to children, and to the children of children, with the aim of demonstrating what reserves of ferocity lie in the depths of the human spirit, and what dangers, today as yesterday, threaten our civilization.'

Primo Levi

11

Miracle in Turin

Primo Levi

[December 1959]

No one expected the success that greeted the Deportation
Exhibition in Turin and the resulting two talks, addressed to
young people, which took place in the premises of the Unione
Culturale [Cultural Union] in the Palazzo Carignano. Not
only the young, but mainly the young, came in very large
numbers, listened with obvious interest, asked thoughtful and
pertinent questions, and on both evenings they then crowded
round those who had been tasked with giving the talks. They
wanted to learn, and also a human contact, something different from their school lessons; the questions they formulated
made obvious their need not just for information about the
facts but for a deeper penetration of the tangle (obscure not
only to them) of the 'hows' and 'whys'.

'Who is responsible for the massacres?' 'How could this
have happened?' 'Why did the Nazi-Fascists exterminate the
Jews?' 'Why, in those desperate situations, did so few defend
themselves?' 'Are there historical precedents for the Lagers?'

Published in *resistenza. Notiziario Gielle* [Resistance: Justice and
Liberty Newsletter] (Turin), 13, 12 (December 1959). The title plays
on that of the film *Miracle in Milan*, scripted by Cesare Zavattini
and directed in 1951 by Vittorio De Sica; in this case, *Miracle in
Turin* refers to the Deportation Exhibition, also the subject of the
previous and following documents.

As one can see, these are very significant questions. Taken together, they seem to indicate a quite well-defined prevailing mind-set, which is that of young people largely ignorant but eager to learn; averse to violence and compromise; more remote than one would expect from the savage world back then, and for that very reason vulnerable and defenceless against whatever savagery and deceit still goes on in the world of today.

It is only an impression, of course, an impression that, moreover, it would be far from easy to extend into a judgement of Italian youth in general. The Palazzo Carignano 'sample' was not an average sample; but it is still important to have been able to see that, alongside the young rebels without a cause and the young layabouts, these honest, attentive and curious young people also exist. What is more, everyone knows how important it is that certain ideas and states of mind should begin to circulate, become established in particular groups and start to take on a life of their own.

It has perhaps been necessary for fifteen years to go by, half a generation, before we could strike the right note in these contacts, but now it seems to all of us that the time is ripe; it is no longer a time to keep silent. The young people at the Palazzo Carignano were promised that more talks would follow; we hope that this long and unnatural silence has been broken once and for all.

12

The Time of the Swastikas

Primo Levi

[1960]

The Deportation Exhibition, which opened in Turin in (it could be said) a minor key, achieved an unexpected success. On every day and at every hour that it was open, a dense and deeply moved crowd stood in front of those terrible images; the closing date even had to be put back twice. Just as surprising was the reception by the Turinese audience of the two resulting talks, intended for young people, which took place in the premises of the Cultural Union at the Palazzo Carignano: a packed, attentive and thoughtful audience. These two outcomes, positive in themselves and worthy of more than superficial attention, contain the hint of a reproach: perhaps we delayed for too long; perhaps we let years be wasted, kept silent when it was time to speak, failed to deliver what was expected of us.

But they also contain a lesson (not a new one, indeed, since, after all, the history of culture is a series of rediscoveries): in this clamorous, mass-media age of ours, full of overt propaganda and hidden persuasion, of mechanical rhetoric, compromises, scandals and ennui, the voice of truth, far from being lost, is acquiring a new tone and a sharper emphasis.

Published in *Il Giornale dei Genitori* [The Parents' Paper] (Turin), 2, 1 (15 January 1960). This article too is inspired by the Deportation Exhibition in Turin in 1959.

It seems too good to be true, but it is so; the widespread devaluation of the word, written and spoken, is not definitive, is not universal; something has been salvaged. Strange as it may seem, even today someone who speaks the truth will be listened to and believed.

This is something to rejoice in; but this manifestation of trust involves an obligation on all of us to examine our conscience. When it comes to the thorny question of how to pass on to our children the heritage of morals and sentiments which we hold to be important, have we not also done wrong? Probably yes, we have done wrong. We have sinned by omission and by commission. In keeping silent, we have sinned out of laziness and through distrusting the power of the word; and when we have spoken, we have often sinned by adopting and accepting a language which is not our own. We all know that the Resistance had its enemies and still does, and they naturally go out of their way to ensure that the Resistance is talked about as little as possible. But I have a suspicion that this suppression also takes place, more or less consciously, through more subtle means – namely, by prematurely embalming the Resistance, relegating it deferentially to the noble castle of the Story of the Nation.

Now, I am afraid that we too may have contributed to this embalming process. In order to describe and transmit the events of yesterday, we have too often adopted a rhetorical language, hagiographic and therefore vague. While there are excellent arguments both for and against describing the Resistance as a 'Second Risorgimento', I ask myself whether it is appropriate to concentrate on this aspect rather than insisting on the fact that the Resistance is still going on, or at any rate should still be going on, since its objectives have been realized only in part. In fact, in this way one finds oneself affirming an ideal continuity between the events of 1848, of 1860, of 1918, and of 1945, at the expense of the much more urgent and obvious continuity between 1945 and today; the interval of twenty years of Fascism comes to lose its significance.

In conclusion, I think that if we want our children to feel these things in order to feel themselves to be our children, we should talk to them a little less about glory and victory, about heroism and sacred soil; and a little more about that tough, hazardous and thankless life, about the daily grind, the days of hope and of despair, about our comrades who died accepting their duty in silence, about involvement of the people (though not all of them) in the errors committed and those avoided, about conspiratorial and military experience painfully acquired through blunders paid for at the cost of human lives, about the difficult (and not spontaneous, and not always perfect) alliance between the ranks of different parties.

Only in this way will the young be able to understand our more recent history as a tissue of human events, and not as a school exercise to add to the many others in the ministerial curriculum.

13

Deposition for the Eichmann Trial

Primo Levi

[1960]

Rome, 14 June 1960

DEPOSITION OF DR PRIMO LEVI, resident of TURIN –
Corso Vittorio 67

On 9 September 1943, along with some friends, I took refuge
in the Val d'Aosta: to be specific, at BRUSSON, above St
Vincent, 54 km from the regional capital.

We had formed a partisan band which included a number
of Jews, among whom I recall GUIDO BACHI, currently
in Paris as the agent of the OLIVETTI company, CESARE

Editors' title. Text of a deposition by Primo Levi, dated 'Rome
14 June 1960' and discovered in Jerusalem in the archives of Yad
Vashem.

This text too was probably recorded and drafted by Massimo
Adolfo Vitale: it was delivered to the aides of Gideon Hausner, the
Attorney General who was preparing the case for the Eichmann
trial, and they passed it on to the Jerusalem Public Prosecutor's
Office with other witness statements by Italian Jews, acquired for
the same purpose. Levi was not summoned to Jerusalem for the
hearing, which began on 11 April 1961 before the District Court
of the city. On 15 December 1961, the defendant was sentenced
to death.

VITA, LUCIANA NISSIM, later married to Momigliano, currently living in Milan and author of the book *Donne contro il mostro* [Women against the Monster], WANDA MAESTRO, deported and deceased in an extermination camp.

We were joined by an individual who went by the name of MEOLI and who, since he was a spy, lost no time in informing on us. With the exception of CESARE VITA, who managed to escape, we were all arrested on 13 September 1943 and taken to AOSTA, to the barracks of the Fascist Militia. There we encountered Centurion FERRO who, knowing that we were all graduates, treated us kindly; he was later killed by the partisans in 1945. I must confess that, as partisans, we were somewhat inexperienced; but no less experienced, it appeared, than the Fascist soldiers who rigged up a sort of trial. Among them there was an Italian from the Alto Adige who spoke perfect German; a certain CAGNI who had already informed on another partisan band; and there was also 'our' MEOLI. They demanded from us the names of other partisans and, above all, those of the leaders. Although we had false identity papers, we declared at once that we were Jews, which proved to be to our advantage at the time, since the search carried out in our rooms was so superficial that they did not even discover the clandestine papers and the revolver which I had hidden in mine. The centurion, having learnt that we were Jews and not 'real partisans', told us: 'You won't come to any harm; we'll send you to the FOSSOLI Camp, near Modena.'

We were given regular rations of the same food as the soldiers, and at the end of January 1944 they took us to Fossoli in a passenger train.

In that camp we were quite well treated; there was no talk of massacres and the atmosphere was peaceful enough; they allowed us to keep the money which we had brought with us and to receive more from outside. We took turns at working in the kitchen and carried out other tasks in the camp; there was even a canteen set up, though in truth a fairly poor one.

At Fossoli I encountered ARTURO FOÀ from Turin, whom we regarded with a certain mistrust, knowing his sympathy for Fascism; all the beggars from the Venice ghetto and the old people from the care home there. I remember a woman called Scaramella and another called USIGLI.

There were also 2 to 300 Yugoslavs and a few English subjects.

When on 18 February we learnt that the German SS had arrived in the village, we were all alarmed, and in fact the next day they informed us that we would be leaving in 24 hours. Nobody tried to escape.

They loaded us into cattle trucks on which were written 'Auschwitz', a name which at that point meant absolutely nothing to us... The journey lasted for three and a half days; we had prepared a collective stock of provisions which we were permitted to take with us. We were 650 Jews...

During the journey, the SS guards showed themselves to be harsh and inhuman; many were savagely beaten. On arrival at Auschwitz, they asked us who was capable of working. Ninety-six of us answered in the affirmative, after which we were driven 7 km to the BUNA MONOWITZ camp; twenty-six women capable of working were transferred to the Birkenau labour camp; all the others were sent to the gas chambers!!!

In our labour camp, there were a number of Jewish doctors. I remember Dr COENKA from Athens, Dr WEISS from Strasbourg, Dr ORENSZTEJN, a Pole who conducted himself very well; I cannot say the same of Dr SAMUELIDIS from Salonica who ignored the patients who turned to him for treatment and informed on the sick to the German SS!!! Several French doctors called LEVY, by contrast, turned out to be fairly humane!

Our squad leader was a Dutch Jew, JOSEF LESSING, an orchestral musician by profession; he had between twenty and sixty men under his orders and, as the one in charge of work squad No. 98, he proved himself to be not only harsh but malevolent.

Among the labourers in that camp, I remember a certain DI PORTO from Rome, a certain PAVONCELLO, LELLO PERUGIA also from Rome, EUGENIO RAVENNA, a shopkeeper, and GIORGIO COHEN from Ferrara, as well as a certain VENEZIA from Trieste who was half Greek. 95% of the labourers in that camp were Jews!! The management of the factory in which I worked was not willing at the time to pay us the wages that were owed to us by law, so it happened that quite a few years after I had returned to my native land, as a result of a class action filed by survivors against the factory, I was granted and paid L. 800,000 as the remuneration to which I was legally entitled!!!

After the arrival of the Soviet troops, we were transferred again to the Auschwitz camp to await the chance to be repatriated.

The odyssey of our return was quite a long one; the Russians told us that they could only repatriate us by sea, embarking at Odessa of all places!!

They transferred us first to Kattowitz, then to Minsk, then to Sluck, and eventually, thank goodness, we got back to Italy.

14

Testimony for Eichmann

Primo Levi

[1961]

Many years have now passed since the end of the Nazi
Lagers. They have been years packed with events for the
world and, for us survivors, years of clarification and decan-
tation. We are therefore able to say things today which,
when just liberated, dazzled, so to speak, by a life regained,
we could not have said clearly. In us, and in everyone, the
initial feelings of outrage, pity and incredulous amazement
have been succeeded by a calmer and more open frame of
mind. Our individual stories, from being chronicles urgently
told, are starting to turn into history.

I think that this is the reason for the renewed interest that
the young are showing in what we have to say; a new atmosphere has come into being, the time is ripe for judgement.

We are glad to affirm that no normal person has taken
sides against us, nobody openly excuses our persecutors of
back then (a few abnormal people, yes – but then they are,
precisely, abnormal). None the less, in the by now numerous
encounters we have had with the public, two objections have
frequently been raised with us. Why are you biased: why do
you tell us about the Nazi Lagers and not about the other
dark chapters of recent history? Or else, more generally, why
do you keep on telling us about these horrors?

Published in *Il Ponte* [The Bridge] (Florence), 17, 4 (April 1961).

The answer to the first objection seems to me to be direct and inescapable: we tell you about the Nazi Lagers because we were there, and because they constitute the most shameful page in human history. Those images which you have seen in exhibitions, including the one here in Turin, are part of our lived experience, they are rooted in our memories, they have affected us; these trials have enriched us, they have turned us into judges. We know that other evils have been committed in the world, and are still being committed; our condemnation extends to all of these evils. That ought to be obvious; whenever we hear of massacres, of tortures, of sealed trains, of suffering gratuitously inflicted on the innocent, of deliberate injustice, the news concerns us and arouses our sympathy: our condemnation extends to all these things. Anyone who returns to tell of the mass murders of women and children, at whoever's hands, in whatever land, in the name of whatever ideology, is our brother, and we are in solidarity with him.

But it is our duty to bear witness in the first place to what we have seen, which brings us to the second objection. Why do we go on talking about atrocities? Are they not over and done with? Have the Germans of today not shown that they have repudiated their past? Why sow more hatred? Why trouble the consciences of our children?

Questions of this kind often spring from bad faith or a questionable conscience, but not always; and in any case, one might respond in many ways. One might justly claim that we have to describe what we have seen in order that moral consciousness may remain alert in everyone, so that, by its opposition, it may build such a barrier that any future attempt is stifled in embryo, so that never again will we hear talk of extermination. One might also justly mention that these inconceivable crimes have been redressed only in part, that many of those responsible have avoided any sanctions, and have only by chance fallen into the nets of an inattentive justice; that the survivors themselves, and the countless families of the victims, have received no recognition, or only a derisory amount of aid or compensation.

But I do not think that this gets to the heart of the matter. I think that even in a world miraculously re-established on the basis of justice, even in a world in which, let us imagine, there was no longer any threat to peace, all violence had disappeared, every offence had been redressed, and every guilty person had been punished and made amends – even in that world, so distant from our own, it would be wrong and foolish to keep silent about the past. History must not be mutilated. There have been events which are too significant, we have observed the symptoms of a disease which is too serious for it to be permissible to keep silent.

Just think: no more than twenty years ago, in the heart of this civilized Europe, there was dreamed an insane dream, that of building a thousand-year empire upon millions of corpses and slaves. The word was proclaimed in the public squares; a very few rejected it and were crushed; all the rest assented, some with revulsion, some with indifference, some with enthusiasm. It was not merely a dream; the empire, an ephemeral empire, was built, and indeed there were corpses and slaves.

Camps were constructed which differed from anything that humankind had devised up until then: they were called labour camps, or even re-education camps, but they had the express purpose of causing the inmates to die, and to die a painful death. But later, Germany gets its hands on what Eichmann calls 'the biological source of Judaism' (note the zoological jargon: the Jews are a race of animals, they are insects, they are a virus, they appear human only by chance, because of a strange freak of nature); and so it is necessary to devise something faster, more industrial.

And here are the compliant German technicians at work; here are the gas chambers being planned and constructed; here is the ideal poison, economical and effective. It is a gas originally meant to destroy rats in ships' holds, and it is ordered in bewildering quantities by an arm of the SS from IG Farbenindustrie. IG Farben diligently fulfil the orders and collect the proceeds, without concerning themselves about anything else. Is there an invasion of rats going on? Better not to ask in order not to know. The German industrialists salve their consciences and profit from the poison.

The firm of Topf and Sons of Erfurt, Constructions in Iron (the name plates are still there on the ovens at Buchenwald, though not on those at Auschwitz, which were blown up), accept the order for a cremation plant capable of destroying 1,000 corpses an hour. The plant is designed, constructed, tested out in the presence of the chief engineer of the firm of Topf and Sons; it is put into operation at the beginning of 1943 and works at full capacity up until October 1944. Calculate the numbers. But there was yet more and worse: there was the shameless demonstration of how easily evil prevails. This, mark well, not only in Germany but wherever the Germans set foot; everywhere, they showed that it is child's play to find traitors and turn them into satraps, to corrupt consciences, to create or restore that atmosphere of equivocal consent or of open terror which was needed to translate their plans into action.

It was like that in France under German domination, in the France that had always been an enemy; it was like that in free and steadfast Norway; it was like that in the Ukraine, in spite of twenty years of Soviet order; and, horrible to relate, the same things happened even in the Polish ghettos, even in the Lagers. It was the gushing out of a flood of violence, fraud and servitude which no dam could withstand, apart from the sporadic islands of the European Resistance.

Even in the Lagers, I have said. We must not retreat from facing the truth, we must not indulge in rhetoric, if we truly want to immunize ourselves. As well as being places of torment and death, the Lagers were places of perdition. Never has the human conscience been violated, wounded and distorted as it was in the Lagers; nowhere has the demonstration to which I referred earlier been more crushing in its proof of the frailty of every conscience and of how easy it is to subvert and overwhelm it. No wonder that a philosopher, Jaspers, and a poet, Thomas Mann, gave up trying to make sense of Hitlerism in rational terms and talked, quite literally, about 'dämonische Mächte': demonic power.

From this perspective, many otherwise puzzling details of the concentrationary method begin to make sense. Humiliating, degrading, reducing a man to the level of his entrails. For this reason, the journeys in sealed wagons, purposely crowded together, purposely deprived of water (there is no question here of economic reasons). For this reason, the yellow star on the breast, the cropping of the hair, even of the women. For this reason, the tattoo, the clumsy clothing, the shoes which make you lame. For this reason – and there is no other way of understanding it – the characteristic, favourite daily ceremony of the march, at a military pace, of those vestiges of men in front of the orchestra, a sight more grotesque than tragic. As well as our masters, the spectators used to include detachments of the Hitlerjugend, boys from 14 to 18 years old, and it is obvious what their impressions must have been. Can these be the Jews they have told us about, the communists, the enemies of our country? But these are not human beings, they are puppets, they are animals; they are filthy and dressed in rags, they don't wash, if you hit them they don't stand up for themselves, they don't fight back; they think about nothing but filling their bellies. It is right to work them to death, it is right to kill them. It is ridiculous to compare them to us, to apply our laws to them.

There was another means of arriving at the same goal of degradation and debasement. The functionaries of the Auschwitz camp, even the highest-ranking ones, were prisoners; many were Jews. One should not suppose that this mitigated the conditions of the camp: on the contrary. It was a selection in reverse: the basest, the most violent, the worst were chosen and given unlimited power, food, clothing, exemption from work, even exemption from death by gas, provided they collaborated. They did collaborate; and so now Commandant Höss can relieve himself of any remorse, he can hold up his hand and say, 'it is clean': we are no more dirty than you, our own slaves worked with us. Reread the terrible page in Höss's diary which talks about the Sonderkommando, the squad assigned to the gas chambers and the crematories, and you will understand what the contagion of evil is.

But that contagion was not only in one direction. To have thought of building a country, indeed a world, on these foundations was not only an abomination but also a bestial madness. It was madness to dream of a nation of overlords, adorned with all the manly qualities of the Germanic Olympus and served by a host of starving and brutalized slaves.

Nothing in Germany was more corrupt and foul than the SS and the organs of the Party. Rumours about the extermination of the Jews, the Poles and the Russians, and of the mentally handicapped in Germany itself, began to spread among the populace and in the army, and this contributed (apart from any moral judgement) to an atmosphere of distrust and dissension around National Socialism, an atmosphere also due to a certain extent to military reverses and to the crumbling of the Axis and its system of alliances. The Germans do not willingly invite allied leaders to view the death installations, yet nevertheless the news spreads: the Germans gain the appearance of being dangerous allies as well as unstable ones. All the Italian troops who come back from the Russian front talk with horror about the scenes they have witnessed, the mass graves, the children and women hunted through the camps like wild animals, whole trains full of Russian prisoners left to die of cold and hunger.

In this way, the cycle reaches its close. The consciousness of fighting for a vile cause unnerves the combatants; more and more German soldiers, though characteristically they continue to serve, feel as a bitter irony the motto, 'God is with us', which they wear on their belts. This is not the cause of the disaster, but it contributes to the disaster.

Everyone knows that History is not always just, that Providence does not always act. On the other hand, everyone loves justice. Why should we hide from our children this striking example of historic justice? Why not tell them the truth, that Hitler created the death camps and was destroyed, and that perhaps he was destroyed precisely for this reason, for having wanted to create the civilization of death?

15

Deportation and Extermination of the Jews

Primo Levi

[1961]

When the racial laws were proclaimed, I was 19 years old. I was enrolled in the first year of chemistry in Turin [University]. A providential and mysterious temporary provision nevertheless allowed me to complete my studies. I must confess that I did not feel ill at ease in the suffocating university environment of that time. Among the students, enthusiastic Fascists were few and for the most part not a danger. Even they were left somewhat perplexed by these new laws, which appeared right from the start to be a stupid aping of the similar and far more savage German laws; but a general scepticism prevailed, by which I too was infected; it was a climate of deafness and blindness to which everyone succumbed, students and

Published in *Storia dell'antifascismo italiano* [History of Italian Anti-Fascism], ed. Luigi Arbizzani and Alberto Caltabiano (Rome: Editori Riuniti, 1964), vol. II, *Testimonianze* [Testimonies].

In 1961, Levi was invited to speak by the committee organizing the celebrations of the centenary of the Unification of Italy in the city of Bologna, which had arranged a series of twelve weekly lectures, taking place at the Teatro Comunale (Communal Theatre). His talk took place on 13 March; that evening, another famous Italian writer of Jewish descent also gave his testimony ('The Fascist Assault on the Ferrara Synagogue'): Giorgio Bassani, the author of *The Garden of the Finzi-Contini*.

professors, Fascists and anti-Fascists and victims of Fascism. You could tell that the war was coming, and the war did come; but for us things did not change very much. I was able to continue my studies in the midst of small and large legal vexations which, however, it was not hard to evade.

From my fellow students and my professors I did not encounter manifestations either of solidarity or of hostility. None the less, Aryan friendships began to melt away one by one, apart from the very few who were not afraid to pass for 'pietists'[1] or 'honorary Jews', as the official Fascist terminology put it. Yet privately even the little hierarchs of the GUF [University Fascist Group] used to look at us with a certain air of guilty embarrassment.

I received my degree in 1941 with the highest marks on my course. I have often thought that these marks, only partly deserved, constituted an extremely cautious and timid act of non-conformity on the part of my professors. None of them, however, had accepted me as a research student; that would have been too grave an imprudence.

During those years, I must admit that the idea of active opposition had not even occurred either to me or to the other young people in my situation. Fascism had had its effect on us; though it had not managed to win over our consciences, it had managed to put them to sleep. It had boasted of its profound influence on social values, but really it had promoted a very serious slackening of them, a general and individual moral vacancy. We professed to be anti-Fascists, but our links with the previous democratic generation had been severed. We lived from day to day, studying, working and having political discussions: academic but sterile and unrealistic.

I found a job in Milan quite easily, since many young men were in the army and a shortage of technicians was making itself felt. Things changed abruptly in 1943. First, there were the workers' strikes in Turin in March: an unheard-of piece of news, a strike in the midst of Fascism, in the middle of

[1] Editors' note: In Fascist terminology, 'pietism' has nothing to do with the religious movement originating in Germany in the late seventeenth century. It denotes excessive sympathy, a tendency to pity the lot of one's enemies, a weakness of character which ought not to infect a genuine Fascist.

the war. There was a strangely timid reaction on the part of the government. One could no longer keep one's eyes shut; something different, something non-conformist and out of line was happening at last; it was not true that in Italy, apart from Fascism, there was a vacuum.

The confirmation came five months later, on 25 July, with the unbelievable, meteoric collapse of the government and of the structures of Fascism. There followed hectic weeks: the Socialist Party, the Communist Party, the Action Party, the Liberal Party, addresses and programmes, new names and new things; the urgent need to make a choice together with a lack of criteria for making a choice; and at the same time the Germans at the Brenner Pass, the Germans on home soil, and the equivocal words of Badoglio: 'The war goes on.'

The catastrophe, foreseen but still unexpected, came on 8 September, and it was utterly crushing. We watched in silence the immediate, terrifying irruption of the German war machine onto the streets of Milan. I lost touch with everyone. Without any definite plan, I returned to Turin and reached the Val d'Aosta. I had no doubt that action was needed, but, despite all the words I had listened to and even spoken, I had extremely confused ideas about what it should be. Other young people flocked to those mountains: draft evaders, disbanded soldiers, workers and local valley-dwellers. We formed ourselves into a band. We managed to establish occasional contacts with the centres of the Resistance which were being organized in Turin, but we had neither money nor weapons nor experience.

Directly after this, on 13 December, as a consequence of our being informed on, a large-scale round-up operation by the Fascist militia caught us completely off guard. Many of us managed to escape; I was captured. I had false documents and I might perhaps have been able to conceal the fact that I was a Jew. However, I admitted it during the second or third interrogation. It was certainly a gross error on my part when judged with the benefit of hindsight, but at that moment I thought it was the best justification for my having taken to the *maquis*. And besides, it seemed to me dishonourable in a way to deny my origins (as you can see, I was very young and foolish!).

I was sent to Fossoli, to which all the other Jews who were captured in the North of Italy gradually streamed in.

There were men, women and children; the healthy, the sick and the dying; millionaires and beggars; all of them waiting for something terrible; but nobody then foresaw what was to follow. When there were 650 of us, the SS made their appearance and announced that in two days' time we would be leaving – all of us, without exception. Where to? Nobody knew. The journey lasted for three days. I think that there is no need to describe a journey of three days in a sealed wagon: cold, thirst, exhaustion, lack of sleep and, above all, terror.

We arrived at night in a far-off place. None of us knew the significance of that name: Auschwitz. We were made to get out of the wagons and questioned briefly: 'Are you healthy? Are you able to work?' On the basis of the replies and of an extremely perfunctory examination, they divided us into three groups: able-bodied men: 96 (of whom I was one); able-bodied women: 29; lastly, all the others. The women set off on foot to the Birkenau camp. Out of the 29, 4 returned. We were taken to the Monowitz camp: 10 of us returned. Out of all the others, the unfit-to-work, no one returned. They were the old, the sick, the children, and the mothers who had not been willing to abandon their children. We learned about it a long time later; they were packed into the gas chambers and burned in the crematory ovens. It was for this that Auschwitz existed; this was the purpose of Auschwitz. So, out of 650, 14 of us returned.

The Monowitz Lager, to which we men were sent, formed part of the group of camps under the authority of Auschwitz, and was 7 kilometres from the main camp. I should say at once that, at that time, this was one of the less harsh camps. The most senior prisoners, who had seen far worse times, mockingly called it the *Sanatorium*. There were no humanitarian reasons for this: the National Socialist system did not recognize such reasons. However, there were others. The Monowitz Lager formed part of a gigantic building site on which an industrial complex was being constructed for I.G. Farben, the major German chemical trust. It was an immense building site, 3 kilometres by 2. The Lager was an integral part of it, even territorially speaking: it was enclosed within the perimeter of the factory. 40,000 labourers worked on the building site. We, the slaves of Monowitz, were 10,000 of these. This was neither an exception nor a secret from anyone: our labour, our contribution to the labour, was an official part of German labour plans and was allowed for in the estimates for the job; and besides, we found ourselves in contact every day on the building site with German civilians, those same German civilians who today know nothing and remember nothing. Our work was remunerated, but not to us; for every day's work, Farben paid 6 marks to our masters, the SS, under whose authority we were.

I am often asked how much of cold calculation there was in these arrangements and how much of insanity and sadism. It was obvious that from the point of view of the SS our services did not represent more than an extra, a side-product of a different business, which was the business of extermination. For it is clear that no industrialist – what am I saying? no slave driver, no captain of galley-slaves in the time of the Pharaohs – could ever have seriously considered turning an economic profit from workers like us. We were almost all assigned to heavy labour, digging and carrying, but we had less strength than a child, and the great majority of us had never picked up a shovel in the whole of our previous lives. Some, a very few, who were in possession of a useful specialism, for example electricians, mechanics, chemists, etc., were given lighter work, but everyone can understand how productive an engineer can be who is chronically hungry, who is dressed in rags, who is covered with infected sores and fleas, who is dirty because he never washes, who is bound to die within a few months and knows it, who knows that perhaps he will be killed the very next day, and who, finally, does not have, and cannot have, any love for or interest in his work – indeed hates it, because it is the work of his mortal enemies.

It is not easy to find words to explain what it means to live in a concentration camp. Still less easy to do so briefly. One can say hunger, but it is a different thing from the hunger that everyone knows, it is a hunger which has become chronic and no longer resides in the belly but in the brain, it has become an obsession, one does not forget it for a single moment of the day; and at night, from the beginning to the end of sleep, one dreams of nothing but eating – or, rather, one dreams that one is about to eat, but then, as in the myth of Tantalus, something, at the last minute, makes the food disappear. One can say exhaustion, but in everyday life no

one experiences exhaustion like this, which is that of a beast
of burden, it is exhaustion with added contempt, exhaustion
without escape and without mercy on the part of those who
impose it, exhaustion accompanied by a sense of pointless-
ness, bestial and debilitating and deprived of all purpose. One
can say cold, but here even the humblest beggar is able to
wrap himself up in some rags and find a warm resting-place
and a glass of wine. In the Lager there is no shelter, one has
to pass the whole of the very long working day dressed in
thin cloth in the midst of the snow, in a climate that is not
like our own, or under the rain, and the blood in one's veins
is cold and impoverished and offers no protection. Consequently hunger, cold and exhaustion lead fatally to disease.
There is an infirmary in the Lager – the *Krankenbau* – but it
only has two medicines, aspirin and urotropine, for all minor
conditions; and for critical diseases, and also for those that
are not critical but incurable – such as hunger oedema, which
is universal – there is a single but radical medicine, and everyone knows it. This is 'the chimney', as it is simply called: it
is the oven at Birkenau.

Yet the rare moments of respite, of the absence of physical
pain and discomfort, such as, for instance, the exceptional
days of rest (I only had five of them in a year), are full of
another kind of pain, no less agonizing: it is the human pain
which springs from the return to awareness, from regain-
ing the perception of how far away one's home is and how
improbable freedom is, from the memory of loved ones, alive
but inaccessible, or else sent to their deaths like beasts to the
slaughter.

Monowitz was none the less a good camp; I say this
without irony. At Monowitz the average life expectancy was
three months because it was an *Arbeitslager*: a labour camp
and not, strictly speaking, an extermination camp. In the
camps of Chelmno, of Sobibor, of Treblinka and of Maj-
danek, by contrast, the average life expectancy was one or
two weeks. If these places are not talked about, it is because
not a single Jew returned from them to tell his story.

I was at Monowitz for a year, and I left it alive through a
combination of providential circumstances. In the first place,
I have always needed little food, so the rations in the Lager,
although not sufficient, were not as appallingly inadequate

for me as they were for many others. One must observe, in fact, that it was precisely the strongest and the most athletic individuals who were the first victims of starvation. I saw very sturdy farm workers from Hungary and Transylvania become reduced to skeletons in a month and take the road to the 'chimney'. Moreover, I had had a good training in mountaineering, and perhaps this is the reason I was able to withstand cold, discomfort and exhaustion without falling ill. I knew a little German and I forced myself, right from the first few days, to learn as much of it as possible.

Here I must open a parenthesis and mention how much the linguistic chaos which dominated it contributed to that inferno. It was an onslaught of orders, threats and curses yelled in German or Polish; of regulations, prohibitions and bizarre rules, some of them positively grotesque, which it was necessary to comprehend or to guess at in an instant. It is no exaggeration to say that it was their ignorance of these languages which caused the very high mortality rate of the Greeks, the French and the Italians in the concentration camp. And it was not easy to guess, for example, that the hail of punches and kicks which had suddenly knocked you to the ground was due to the fact that the buttons on your jacket numbered four, or six, instead of five, or that you had been seen in bed, in the middle of winter, with a hat on your head.

Knowing German was providential for me in quite another way too. In June of 1944, the Germans at Farben needed chemists for their laboratories. Many of us put ourselves forward – too many. It was necessary to establish who was a chemist and who was not. The Germans are 'serious people' and organized a serious examination, in German naturally. That the candidates were living spectres who found it hard to stay on their feet did not concern them in the least; what did concern them was production and hence the finding of presumably useful technicians. They found three and I was one of them.

I do not think that I was very useful to Farben. Those were months of incessant air raids on account of which my work as a *spezialist* was limited to carrying the fragile measuring instruments three or four times a day from the laboratory to the cellar and vice versa. But, above all, I did not have the slightest intention of making myself useful. At all events, this was how I had the rare privilege of passing the freezing months of the winter of 1944–45 under cover and in the warm, and without having to work excessively hard.

In addition, I owe my salvation to a final miraculous intervention of fate. As I have mentioned, I never had an illness of any kind during my year in the Lager, but around 10 January 1945, when the Russian artillery could already be heard, I fell ill with scarlet fever and was admitted to the camp infirmary. A few days later, the entire camp was evacuated, and simultaneously all the camps in Upper Silesia were evacuated, Auschwitz included. This is perhaps the most terrible and the least well-known chapter in the history of Auschwitz. The operation, which seems to have been decided on by Hitler in person, took place in a few hours: all the prisoners able to walk – and there were more than 150,000 in the Auschwitz area – were forced to set off through the snow, in the bitter cold, without food, without rest, for seven days and seven nights, towards Mauthausen, Buchenwald and Dachau; it is hundreds of kilometres, which had to be covered along roads congested with disbanded soldiers, fleeing civilians and columns of troops on the march.

There were two reasons for this insane march: to salvage workers for an imaginary counter-offensive, and not to leave witnesses behind. For this reason, no one was left behind alive. Anyone who delayed the march was put down. No more than a tenth survived that horrifying deportation within the deportation. And these were admitted to the other lagers I have named – which were already impossibly crowded – and had to start work again immediately. I remained with the sick in the Monowitz infirmary, and so I was spared this hellish adventure.

The SS had had orders to set fire to our huts and to machine-gun anyone who tried to escape. They were just about to carry out the order when a violent air raid devastated the camp. By the end of the air raid, the Germans had fled. We invalids stayed there for ten days, left to ourselves without food or medical treatment in the damaged huts. More than half had died from starvation or disease when the Russians arrived on 27 January 1945.

16

Statement for the Bosshammer Trial

Primo Levi

[1965]

5 December 1965

Preparations for the transports. I was sent to the Fossoli camp on 27 January 1944. The camp was under the control of the Italian Pubblica Sicurezza [Public Security police]; when I arrived, it held about 350 Italian and foreign Jews. On around 15 February, about 10 soldiers of the German SS arrived at Fossoli, among them a German warrant officer, also in the SS; he took over command from the Italian officers and directly organized the deportation. We were told through interpreters that all the Jews would be leaving for a cold country, so it was advisable to take with us heavy clothing, blankets and furs, in addition, of course, to valuables and

---

Editors' title. A typed page with a handwritten signature and with the note 'Testimony given to the Centro di Documentazione Ebraica Contemporanea [Centre for Contemporary Jewish Research] on 5 December 1965'. The document is preserved in Milan in the CDEC Archive.

In 1964, the Court of Dortmund approached the CDEC during the judicial inquiry into ex-Sturmbannführer (colonel) of the SS Friedrich Bosshammer, direct collaborator with Eichmann, accused of the deportation of 3,500 Italian Jews. Levi's text was used in the preliminary phase of the trial.

money. The deportation took place when the number of Jews present had reached 650; even those very seriously ill were deported, including a dying woman in her nineties. However, those with infectious diseases were left in Italy, along with a few Jews of English nationality. No provisions for the journey were prepared or handed out by the Germans, but we were allowed to buy them in the camp.

We were transported from the camp to the railway station on 22 February 1944 in buses driven by Italian personnel, but escorted by the German soldiers mentioned above; these behaved with great brutality, striking us with punches and kicks to speed up the boarding and descent from the motor vehicles, and the entry into the wagons. No receptacles had been put inside the wagons themselves (goods wagons of the sealed variety) either for water or for sanitary requirements; the floor was covered with a thin layer of straw.

I believe that this was the first transport of Jews from Fossoli to Germany; it left Fossoli on 22/2 and arrived at Auschwitz on the evening of 26/2.

Escort on the journey. This was made up of Germans in SS uniform, at least two of whom were among the ten mentioned above.

Destination of the transport. This was clearly indicated ('Auschwitz') on a sign stuck into a frame on the outside of every wagon.

Among the Pubblica Sicurezza officers responsible for overseeing and administering the Fossoli camp, I remember the following names: Avitabile, Tedesco, Taglialatela. They behaved towards us with decency and humanity; I think that they may know and remember the names of the Germans in charge of the deportation of our convoy.

17

The Deportation of the Jews

Primo Levi

[1966]

Round about 8 September, since I was a Jew and therefore excluded from the army and the universities, I joined a partisan band. We encountered droves of Italian soldiers, coming from France and from the whole of Italy, who were making the opposite journey, some on their way home and some in search of weapons or of a leader.

All the ex-soldiers with whom we talked had only one thing to say, that one should no longer fight alongside the Germans because they had seen what they had done; they had been at the front in Greece, in Yugoslavia, in Russia and they said: 'This is not war, these are not allies, they are not soldiers, they are not men'. The bond which united us was born from this very human evidence of the pure and simple humanity which, despite the many failings of the Italians, still survives in Italy. This, it seems to me, is the first factor

---

Published in *Quaderni del Centro di Studi sulla deportazione e l'internamento* [Notebooks of the Centre for Deportation and Internment Studies] (Rome), 4 (1967). Talk delivered on the occasion of the national congress of the Associazione ex internati (Association of Ex-Internees), held in Turin from 22 to 24 October 1966.

not to be overlooked in describing the contribution of the military internees.

The second is this: although I was captured as a partisan, I foolishly, or through lack of awareness – whichever you want to call it – declared myself to be a Jew, and ended up in the Auschwitz camp.

The labour camp where I worked was close to one in which there were Englishmen and Americans, Russian, Polish and French prisoners and also Italian prisoners; some were soldiers, others were rounded-up civilians, and yet others so-called 'voluntary workers'. The Italian prisoners were not much better off than us; it is true that in their camp there were no gas chambers or crematories and this is a very important detail, but, for one thing, their basic living conditions and clothing were not very different from ours.

However, in the case of those Italian soldiers who found themselves in better conditions because they were 'specialist workers' and had a trade, we had help from all of them, and not only from them but also from the civilian Italian prisoners; and it was not only us Italians that they recognized in this way, but everyone. It was touching, the kind-heartedness of those fellow countrymen of ours. The Germans knew that the Italians were 'decent people' as they used to say in sneering tones, and it was true, it was common knowledge. I believe that this concurs with the fact which has been talked about at length this evening, namely the high percentage – almost the entirety – of Italian troops who refused to support the RSI [Italian Social Republic] because that would mean supporting Nazism and the inhumanity of the Nazi system.

That said, and even though I was arrested as a partisan, I bring here this evening the testimony of all those who had no choice, whereas for the young, for the young of my generation, there was in fact a choice (and in my case, there was one later), the choice to say *no*, to refuse to comply.

I bring the testimony of those who had no choice, which is to say of all Jewish citizens, Italian and foreign. These had no choice at all; they were women, they were old, they were people cut off for years by then from any contact with the outside world, who had been living a clandestine life since 1939, and for them a choice was clearly impossible. I should say *almost* impossible, because in spite of everything, in spite of the immense difficulties, in spite of the lack of an organization, there was still a resistance, not only within the Polish, Russian and Ukrainian Jewish minorities but even inside the concentration camps themselves: groups would join in coalition and collaboration with the other clandestine movements which sprang up and survived in all the concentration camps.

Naturally, it was a different matter for those in concentration camps for political prisoners than it was for those who, on the contrary, were in concentration camps like Auschwitz, in which the majority were Jewish; the reasons are obvious: in a camp where all or the majority were political prisoners, those prisoners had behind them a political training acquired in a very hard school. Besides which, they were men at the peak of their physical strength, many of whom had been deported in the middle of a normal working life. In addition, it was easy for solidarity to exist, at least within national groups and also through political affinities. In the Auschwitz camp things were different; it was a Babel, at least for us Italians, it was being hurled into the dark: that is to say, cast into an unknown world which we could not understand. We could not understand for many reasons; for one thing, because of the language, and also because the camp was governed by a rigid set of regulations which no one taught us about and which we had to learn by intuition, barely able to communicate, making mistakes and dying. And also because the mosaic of nationalities, origins and ideologies was so complicated and confusing that one would really have needed months to get one's bearings, and within months one was dead.

At Auschwitz, 95% were Jews and about 5% were political prisoners or the so-called green triangles, which is to say common criminals. Legally, this made no difference, but in reality there was a difference and it was a vast one: the political prisoners and the 'green triangles' were nearly all German, and the Germans themselves never forgot this. Even the German communists, most of whom had been exterminated by Hitler, were regarded, because of their race and language, as profoundly different from the Jews. The German political prisoners, who often treated us very well, had been prisoners for five, ten or twelve years and they all knew what it meant to 'work your way up'; they had done that: anyone who had not was no longer alive. So, despite the regulations, even if they were not entitled to different treatment, they received it or organized it for themselves.

The average life expectancy of the camp that I was in, which was a good one because it was a labour camp, was three months; in three months the population would be reduced by half, though it would be replenished by new intakes. I have called it a good camp for many reasons: because it was a labour camp, and because there were many opportunities to make contact with Italian military internees and even with English ones; the barrier which separated us from the world was not completely impermeable: there were a few gaps, a few loopholes. But everyone knows what kind of camp Birkenau was: it was a camp from which no one escaped, where there was no question of average life expectancy; its only purpose was to destroy.

I am not saying this in order to establish some kind of precedence or aristocracy among internees; far be it from me to have any such intention. I simply wanted to point out that even under these conditions, even in the Auschwitz camp, a resistance movement was born, and not just a clandestine one, since it came to light through an episode which is still unknown to history – since there were no survivors – namely the sabotage of the crematory ovens.

It is to be hoped that it will somehow be possible, on the basis of a few surviving witnesses and of investigations on the ground, to clarify fully how this took place. Under those conditions of *zero*, of nothing, still a group of people were able not only, first of all, to blow up the crematory ovens, but also to get hold of weapons, to fight with the Germans, to kill several of them, and to make an escape attempt.

It also deserves to be remembered that about thirty men succeeded in getting past the perimeter, only to be handed over to the Germans by the Poles, who themselves were mad with terror of the Germans. And so, these few dozen heroes, who succeeded for the first time in creating a way out of Auschwitz which might have served not only for them but for the entire population of the camp, saw their attempt fail miserably.

18

Questionnaire for the Bosshammer Trial

Leonardo De Benedetti

[1970]

Fragebogen / Questionnaire

(1) *Wo lebten Sie bis zu Ihrer Verhaftung in Italien?*
Where did you live before your arrest in Italy?

In Turin

(2) *Wann und von wem wurden Sie verhaftet?*
When and by whom were you arrested?

on 3-XII-'43 at Lanzo d'Intelvi (Como) by the Fascist Militia at the Swiss frontier; I had been turned back from Switzerland, where I had tried to take refuge along with my wife

(3) *Warum werden Sie verhaftet?*
Why were you arrested?

The document, six typed pages with a handwritten signature and dated 5 August 1970, is preserved in Milan in the CDEC Archive.

The 'Fragebogen / Questionnaire' was sent by the Court of West Berlin (to which the trial had been transferred in 1969) to the Italian witnesses approached during the preliminary investigation. The questions were given in both German and Italian.

because Jewish

(4) *Wohin kamen Sie nach Ihrer Verhaftung?*
Where were you transported after your arrest?

First to the Como prison, then to the one in Modena and then to the Fossoli Concentration Camp

(5) *Waren Sie im Polizei-Durchgangslager Fossoli di Carpi (bei Modena)?*
Were you in the police transit camp at Fossoli di Carpi (near Modena)?
Wenn ja, wann und von wo aus kamen Sie dorthin und wie lange blieben Sie in Fossoli?
If this is the case, when and from where were you transported there, and how long did you stay there?

Period in the Fossoli Camp: from 21-XII-'43 to 21-II-'44

Wie wurden Sie und Ihre Leidensgenossen dort behandelt?
How were you and your companions in misfortune treated there?

Not too badly as long as the Camp remained under the management of the Italian Police, which is to say up until two days before the departure to Auschwitz

(6) *Haben Sie in Italien den damaligen SS-Sturmbannführer Friedrich Boßhammer kennengelernt?*
Did you meet Friedrich Bosshammer, ex-Sturmbannführer of the SS, in Italy?

I do not know; we never knew the names of the SS officers and soldiers.

Falls ja, bei welcher Gelegenheit und unter welchen Umständen?
If this is the case: on what occasion and under what circumstances did you meet him?

(7) *Wann sind Sie aus Fossoli di Carpi (oder gegebenenfalls aus einen anderen Ort Italiens) nach Auschwitz*

deportiert worden (Daten bitte so genau wie möglich angeben)?
When were you deported from Fossoli di Carpi (or, if that is the case, from elsewhere in Italy) to Auschwitz? (Please give the date as accurately as possible)?

Departed from Fossoli the evening of 21-II-'44, arrived at Auschwitz the evening of 26-II-'44

(8) *Wußten Sie bei Ihrem Abtransport aus Italien, wohin Sie gebracht wurden?*
On departure from Italy, did you know to where you were being transported?

Yes, to Auschwitz

(9) *War Ihnen <u>vor</u> Ihrer Deportation bekannt, daß den deportierten Juden der Tod drohte oder hegten Sie mindestens entsprechende Befürchtungen?*
<u>Before</u> your deportation, did you know that the Jews were threatened with death, or did you at least fear it?

I knew it for certain

Falls ja, wie kamen Sie zu Ihrem Wissen oder wodurch wurden Ihre Befürchtungen hervorgerufen?
If this is the case: how did you come to know it and what was it that caused your fear?

Information from Yugoslav, German, Polish and Austrian Jews, refugees in Italy, who were fully aware of what was happening in the German Concentration Camps

(10) *Wie kamen Sie nach Auschwitz (Art des Abtransportes, Ein- und Ausladebahnhof, Fahrtroute des Zuges usw.)?*
How were you transported to Auschwitz (mode of transport, stations where you were loaded and unloaded, itinerary of the train etc.)?

By train, freight wagons, 40–50 people in each wagon, without pallets or blankets. Itinerary: Fossoli – Brenner Pass – Vienna – Morawska Ostrawa – Auschwitz

(11) *Wie lange waren Sie von Italien nach Auschwitz unterwegs?*
How long were you in transit from Italy to Auschwitz?

Five days

(12) *Schildern Sie bitte die näheren Umständs Ihrer Fahrt nach Auschwitz (Personen- oder Güterwagen, Belegung Ihres Waggons, Verpflegungsausgabe, etwa warmes Essen und Getränke bei Antritt und während der Fahrt, Aussteigemöglichkeiten bei Zwischenaufenthalten, Todesfälle während der Fahrt usw.).*
Please describe the precise circumstances of your journey to Auschwitz (passenger train – freight train, how many people were there to a wagon, provision of rations, for instance hot food and drink, before and during the journey, possibility of getting off during a stop, deaths during the journey etc.).

No hot food, neither before nor during the journey nor on arrival; as rations, black bread, cheese, a little jam; to drink, cold water distributed with the rations once a day; possibility of getting off the train once a day in open countryside to attend to bodily needs in front of everyone, fellow travellers and the guards; deaths, an old man of 75. Much suffering due to the terrible cold and thirst

(13) *Wie viele Menschen wurden nach Ihrer Schätzung mit Ihrem Transport nach Auschwitz deportiert (Anhaltspunkte fur Ihre Schätzung können die Länge des Zuges, die Anzahl und die Belegung der einzelnen Waggons sowie Ihre Beobachtungen beim Einladen in Italien und Ausladen in Auschwitz sein)?*
According to your estimation, how many people were deported to Auschwitz on the same transport (your estimation can be based, for example, on the length of the train, the number and the degree of occupancy of the individual wagons and also on observations made during loading in Italy and unloading at Auschwitz)?

For certain, my transport was made up of 650 people, the oldest aged 75 (deceased on the journey), the youngest aged three months

(14) *Wo kamen Sie in Auschwitz an und wo wurden Sie ausgeladen?*
Where at Auschwitz did you arrive and where were you unloaded?

Arrived at the Auschwitz railway station at 21 hours on 26-II-'44, the group was immediately divided: on one side the women and children, on the other the men, and then each group subdivided again into 2: Young and healthy on one side, old people and children under 14 and the sick on the other

(15) *Fand eine Selektion statt? Wie ging sie vor sich?*
Was there a selection and in what way was it carried out?

The selection was very quick and brutal: I was put in the group of the healthy, which turned out to be composed of 95 men and was immediately transported in a number of trucks to the Monowitz Labour Camp (known as 'BUNA'); the group of women admitted to the labour Camp (12 women) was taken instead to Birkenau.

(16) *Wie viele Männer und Frauen kamen nach der Selektion zur Arbeitseinsatz im Lager? Was wurde aus den übrigen?*
After the selection, how many men and how many women were deployed to work in the camp? What happened to the others?

95 men and 12 women; all the others were immediately taken to the Gas Chambers in Birkenau and gassed that same evening. Of the 95 men and 12 women admitted into the labour camps, the number who came back to Italy at the end of the war was 8 and 4 respectively.

(17) *Welche Häftlingsnummer erhielten Sie in Auschwitz?*
What inmate number were you given in Auschwitz?

174489

(18) *Wann und wodurch erfuhren Sie, was in Auschwitz mit den Juden geschah?*
When and on what occasion did you find out what was happening to the Jews at Auschwitz?

From the winter of 1942–1943, when I offered my services as a doctor to a Jewish aid organization for foreign Jewish refugees in Italy

(19) *Wie viele Teilnehmer Ihres Transportes haben außer Ihres das Kriegsende uberlebt? Geben Sie bitte gegebenenfalls Namen und Adressen der Ihren bekannten Überlebenden an? Welche Ihnen namentlich bekannten Teilnehmer Ihres Transportes sind in Auschwitz ermordet worden?*
(A) Apart from yourself, how many members of your transport survived the end of the war?
(B) If possible, please give the name and address of survivors of your acquaintance.
(C) How many members known to you by name were murdered in Auschwitz?

(A) 7 men and 4 women

(B) Dr Primo LEVI – Turin – Corso re Umberto 75
Dr Aldo MOSCATI – PISA – Lungarno Buozzi 2
Dr Luciana NISSIM – MILAN – Via ????
Stella VALABREGA – ?????????
Eugenio RAVENNA – FERRARA – Via Bologna
Luciano MARIANI – MILAN (deceased in December 1968)
Leo Zelicowski – ARCO (Trento) – Via Capitelli 49
? ZELICOWICH – ?????

(C) Jolanda DE-BENEDETTI née DE-BENEDETTI from ALBA (Cuneo)
Franco SACERDOTE from Naples
Renato Ortona from Turin
Guido Melli from Modena
Engineer Mario Levi from Milan with wife and daughter

Giuseppe (?) LURIA from Turin
Guido Valabrega from Turin and wife
Enrico MARIANI from Venice with wife, son, father, mother
    and 2 cousins
? GLUKSMANN from Vienna
? ISRAEL and wife from Sarajevo
Signora ? Kabilio
Valabrega family from Genoa (father, mother, son, daughter)
Family of Major BASSANI from Udine (father, mother, son,
    daughter)
Ravenna family from Ferrara (father, mother, daughter)
TEDESCO family from Venice (father, mother, two sons)

Turin – 5-VIII-'70
(date)

Dr Leonardo DE-BENEDETTI
(signature)

1 Js 1/65 (RSHA)

F r a g e b o g e n
Q u e s t i n a r i o

1) Wo lebten Sie bis zu Ihrer Verhaftung in Italien?
   Dove ha vissuto fino al Suo arresto in Italia?

Sempre in Italia, a Torino e a Milano.

2) Wann und von wem wurden Sie verhaftet?
   Quando e da chi è stato arrestato?

Il 13 dicembre 1943, dalla Milizia fascista (Centurione Ferro), presso
BRUSSON (Aosta).

3) Warum wurden Sie verhaftet?
   Perché è stato arrestato?

Per attività partigiana. La mia qualità di ebreo è venuta in luce più tardi.

4) Wohin kamen Sie nach Ihrer Verhaftung?
   Dove è stato trasportato dopo il Suo arresto?

Dapprima alla caserma della Milizia fascista in Aosta, poi (verso la fine di
gennaio 1944) al campo di Fossoli di Carpi.

5) Waren Sie im Polizei-Durchgangslager Fossoli di Carpi
   (bei Modena)?
   È stato nel campo di transito poliziesco di Fossoli di Carpi
   (presso Modena)?
                                   Si.
   Wenn ja, wann und von wo aus kamen Sie dorthin und wie lange
   blieben Sie in Fossoli?
   Se questo è il caso: quando e partendo da che luogo ci è
   stato trasportato, e quanto tempo ci è rimasto?
Da Aosta (vedi sopra): sono rimasto a Fossoli fino al 22 febbraio 1944.

Figure 6 Primo Levi, 'Questionnaire for the Bosshammer Trial', 2
September 1970, first page (Archive of the Centre for Contemporary Jewish Research (CDEC), Milan, Fondo Processo di Berlino,
b. 6, fasc. 56).

19

Questionnaire for the Bosshammer Trial

Primo Levi

[1970]

Fragebogen / Questionnaire

(1) *Wo lebten Sie bis zu Ihrer Verhaftung in Italien?*
Where did you live before your arrest in Italy?

Always in Italy, in Turin and Milan

(2) *Wann und von wem wurden Sie verhaftet?*
When and by whom were you arrested?

13 December 1943, by the fascist Militia (Centurion Ferro) near BRUSSON (Aosta).

(3) *Warum werden Sie verhaftet?*
Why were you arrested?

For partisan activity. My Jewish identity came to light later.

(4) *Wohin kamen Sie nach Ihrer Verhaftung?*
Where were you transported after your arrest?

Six typed pages, numbered, with a handwritten signature and the typed date '2 September 1970'. The document is preserved in Milan in the CDEC Archive.

First to the barracks of the fascist Militia in Aosta, then (towards the end of January 1944) to the Fossoli di Carpi camp.

(5) *Waren Sie im Polizei-Durchgangslager Fossoli di Carpi (bei Modena)?*
Were you in the police transit camp at Fossoli di Carpi (near Modena)?

Yes

Wenn ja, wann und von wo aus kamen Sie dorthin und wie lange blieben Sie in Fossoli?
If this is the case, when and from where were you transported there, and how long did you stay there?

From Aosta (see above); I remained at Fossoli until 22 February 1944.

Wie wurden Sie und Ihre Leidensgenossen dort behandelt?
How were you and your companions in misfortune treated there?

During our time there, the camp was under the administration of the Italian Police. We did not suffer ill treatment, but food was scarce for those without money.

(6) *Haben Sie in Italien den damaligen SS-Sturmbannführer Friedrich Boßhammer kennengelernt?*
Did you meet Friedrich Bosshammer, ex-Sturmbannführer of the SS, in Italy?

No.

Falls ja, bei welcher Gelegenheit und unter welchen Umständen?
If this is the case: on what occasion and under what circumstances did you meet him?

(7) *Wann sind Sie aus Fossoli di Carpi (oder gegebenenfalls aus einen anderen Ort Italiens) nach Auschwitz*

deportiert worden (Daten bitte so genau wie möglich angeben)?
When were you deported from Fossoli di Carpi (or, if that is the case, from elsewhere in Italy) to Auschwitz? (Please give the date as accurately as possible)?

I was deported from Fossoli to Auschwitz on 22 February 1944.

(8) *Wußten Sie bei Ihren Abtransport aus Italien, wohin Sie gebracht wurden?*
On departure from Italy, did you know to where you were being transported?

We were given no information. The wagons of the convoy had signs saying 'Auschwitz'; however, none of us knew where Auschwitz was, and what that name meant.

(9) *War Ihnen vor Ihrer Deportation bekannt, daß den deportierten Juden der Tod drohte oder hegten Sie mindestens entsprechende Befürchtungen?*
Before your deportation, did you know that the Jews were threatened with death, or did you at least fear it?

I feared it.

Falls ja, wie kamen Sie zu Ihrem Wissen oder wodurch wurden Ihre Befürchtungen hervorgerufen?
If this is the case: how did you come to know it and what was it that caused your fear?

From the news on Radio Britannica [Radio London], and from conversations with a number of foreign Jews (especially Croatians) who had taken refuge in Italy to escape the Nazi occupation.

(10) *Wie kamen Sie nach Auschwitz (Art des Abtransportes, Ein- und Ausladebahnhof, Fahrtroute des Zuges usw.)?*
How were you transported to Auschwitz (mode of transport, stations where you were loaded and unloaded, itinerary of the train etc.)?

In freight wagons, from Carpi station to Auschwitz station via Mantua, Verona, the Brenner Pass, Salzburg, Vienna, Brno.

(11) *Wie lange waren Sie von Italien nach Auschwitz unterwegs?*
How long were you in transit from Italy to Auschwitz?

Four days.

(12) *Schildern Sie bitte die näheren Umständs Ihrer Fahrt nach Auschwitz (Personen- oder Güterwagen, Belegung Ihres Waggons, Verpflegungsausgabe, etwa warmes Essen und Getränke bei Antritt und während der Fahrt, Aussteigemöglichkeiten bei Zwischenaufenthalten, Todesfälle während der Fahrt usw.).*
Please describe the precise circumstances of your journey to Auschwitz (passenger train – freight train, how many people were there to a wagon, provision of rations, for instance hot food and drink, before and during the journey, possibility of getting off during a stop, deaths during the journey etc.).

The train was made up of 12 wagons, with 45 to 60 people per wagon. We received neither food nor drink of any kind during the journey; we were only allowed to take bread, jam and water with us. We were permitted to get out of the wagon once a day; we were forbidden to ask for food through the window in stations. To my knowledge, at least one woman died during the journey: it was forbidden to unload the corpse.

(13) *Wie viele Menschen wurden nach Ihrer Schätzung mit Ihrem Transport nach Auschwitz deportiert (Anhaltspunkte fur Ihre Schätzung können die Länge des Zuges, die Anzahl und die Belegung der einzelnen Waggons sowie Ihre Beobachtungen beim Einladen in Italien und Ausladen in Auschwitz sein)?*
According to your estimation, how many people were deported to Auschwitz on the same transport (your estimation can be based, for example, on the length of

the train, the number and the degree of occupancy of the individual wagons and also on observations made during loading in Italy and unloading at Auschwitz)?

The deportees on that convoy were 650.

(14) *Wo kamen Sie in Auschwitz an und wo wurden Sie ausgeladen?*
Where at Auschwitz did you arrive and where were you unloaded?

We got off the train at night, at the station in the city of Auschwitz (not at Birkenau); the selection took place right there.

(15) *Fand eine Selektion statt? Wie ging sie vor sich?*
Was there a selection and in what way was it carried out?

The selection happened immediately, and was very rapid: a glance and a question, 'Are you healthy or ill?' On the basis of the reply, we were pointed in three directions, where three or more trucks were waiting (respectively able-bodied men; able-bodied women; incapacitated).

(16) *Wie viele Männer und Frauen kamen nach der Selektion zur Arbeitseinsatz im Lager? Was wurde aus den übrigen?*
After the selection, how many men and how many women were deployed to work in the camp? What happened to the others?

Sent to work: 69 men (to Monowitz-Buna)
29 women (to Birkenau)
All the others were killed within 2 or 3 days.[1]

(17) *Welche Häftlingsnummer erhielten Sie in Auschwitz?*
What inmate number were you given in Auschwitz?

---

[1] In his answer to question 16, Levi inverts the digits of the number of men selected to work: he wrote on many other occasions that the number was 96 rather than 69, although historical research has established that the number was 95.

174517

(18) *Wann und wodurch erfuhren Sie, was in Auschwitz mit den Juden geschah?*
When and on what occasion did you find out what was happening to the Jews at Auschwitz?

In the Monowitz-Buna camp, from conversations with fellow prisoners.

(19) *Wie viele Teilnehmer Ihres Transportes haben außer Ihres das Kriegsende überlebt? Geben Sie bitte gegebenenfalls Namen und Adressen der Ihren bekannten Überlebenden an? Welche Ihnen namentlich bekannten Teilnehmer Ihres Transportes sind in Auschwitz ermordet worden?*
Apart from yourself, how many members of your transport survived the end of the war?
If possible, please give the name and address of survivors of your acquaintance.
How many members known to you by name were murdered in Auschwitz?

As far as I know, 13 other members of my transport survived. These included:

Leonardo De Benedetti, Re Umberto 61, <u>Turin</u>
Eugenio Ravenna, <u>Ferrara</u>
Liko Israel, Kiryat Tivon, Yizreel Str. 4. <u>Israel</u>
Aldo Moscati, Viale Buozzi 1, <u>Pisa</u>
Luciana Nissim Momigliano, via F. Corridoni 1, <u>Milan</u>

N.B. Further details of my arrest and deportation can be found in my book *Se questo è un uomo* [*If This is a Man*], pub. Einaudi, published also in Germany by Fischer Bucherei of Frankfurt (*Ist das ein Mensch?* 1961).

Primo Levi
(signature)

2 September 1970
(date)

Primo LEVI, corso Re Umberto 75, 10128 <u>TURIN</u>, Italy.

20

Deposition for the Bosshammer Trial

Primo Levi

[1971]

Court of Turin, Monday 3 May 1971

Primo Levi, born in Turin 31.7.1919, resident in Turin, Corso Re Umberto 75.

D.R. 'I am Jewish in the full legal sense of the term.'

D.R. 'If it proves necessary to proceed to a second interrogation, for reasons of work I would prefer to testify in Italy. However, I have no objections in principle to going to Germany.'

I was arrested in December 1943 by the fascist militia, as a consequence of being informed on. The action of the fascist militia was not directed at the capture of Jews, but of a partisan band of which I was a member.

Editors' title. Text of a deposition given in Turin on 3 May 1971 in the office of the investigating judge, Dr Barbaro, to the German state prosecutor Dietrich Hölzner.

Levi spoke for four hours, in Italian and German, with the help of an interpreter. The transcription of his testimony – carried out by hand by Eloisa Ravenna, who from 1964 worked as a historical expert on behalf of the German judicial authorities – is preserved in Milan in the CDEC Archive. Condemned to life imprisonment in April 1972 in the criminal court of West Berlin, Friedrich Bosshammer died a few months after being sentenced.

After my arrest I was interrogated by the militia itself and by the Italian police; in the course of this interrogation I myself declared that I was a Jew. As a consequence of this declaration of mine I was sent to the Fossoli internment camp near Carpi. The transfer to the Fossoli camp took place towards the end of January 1944.

As far as I know, at that time the Fossoli camp was under the administration of the Italian police.

Our relations with the Italian police officers were quite good. In response to our questions, they assured us repeatedly that the camp would remain under Italian administration and that we would not be handed over to the German authorities.

I cannot say precisely when the German authorities took over the running of the camp from the Italian ones; however, I remember having seen the SS for the first time on the day of 20.2.1944; I can vouch for this date because immediately after my return I wrote notes intended for inclusion in a book. This book had the Italian title *Se questo è un uomo* [*If This is a Man*], pub. De Silva, 1947, and was translated into German with the title *Ist das ein Mensch?*, Fischer Bücherei 1961.

On about the 20th, I personally saw for the first time a group of four or five SS – I do not remember the exact number. I can say with certainty that they belonged to the SS, because already at that time I knew the difference between the uniforms of the Wehrmacht and those of the SS. According to the accounts of some of my fellow prisoners, these SS soldiers had already been present in the camp for several days, but I saw them for the first time on about 20 February. I cannot say what their ranks were, but I can confirm that at least one of them was an officer, because I heard him giving orders to the others. I was not able to observe whether he arrived together with the others or not. This officer exchanged a few words in German with us as well; he also occasionally made use of a few Italian words, and I remember having heard him say in Italian, addressing the others, 'Campo grande, legna niente' [Big camp, firewood none]; he meant this as a criticism of the previous administration of the camp. From this phrase of his, we drew some hope about our future fate.

I have been shown some photographs of the accused Bosshammer, but I am not able to recognize in these pictures any of the people I saw back then. As far as I recall, at the time of my arrival at the Fossoli camp there were between 100 and 200 Italian Jews; their number then rapidly increased and reached a total of 650 at the time of the deportation. A little earlier than 20 February, a group of Jews reached Fossoli from the Carceri Nuove [New Prison] in Turin. I am not able to say whether they were brought to Fossoli by the Italians or by the Germans. Nor can I say if it was together with the SS that a group of between 60 and 80 Jews arrived at Fossoli. I cannot say for certain if the arrivals were more frequent in the second half of February, but I remember that, about fifteen days after our arrival, a group of Jews who had just arrived had to sleep on the ground for a night because there was nowhere to accommodate them. As far as I remember, the approximately 400 Jews who came to Fossoli during my stay there did so in groups.

Officially, the administration of the camp had remained in Italian hands, but we immediately had the impression that effective command had passed to the Germans; in fact, that same evening of 20 February, an SS soldier, on being questioned by us, said that we would all be leaving the next day or the day after. These were perhaps the first German words that I heard. The German who pronounced those words was a common soldier.

After the announcement of departure, internal conditions in the camp did not change, but the external guard was reinforced. I cannot say which of the Germans was personally responsible for declaring that if one of us escaped, ten would be shot. On the morning of 21 February, some of us asked the SS soldiers whether we should or could take our possessions with us. They replied that we would be well treated, but that our destination was a cold country; for that reason they advised us to take with us everything we owned, money, gold, jewellery, foreign currency and especially furs, blankets, etc. We asked the SS soldiers where our destination was and what would happen to us, but they replied that they did not know.

I do not remember if family groups were individually questioned; it may be that this happened in the case of non-Italian Jews. However, the SS certainly had a list in alphabetical order, since on the morning of 22 February a roll call took place at which each individual had to reply 'present'. I remember the precise number of the deported Jews, which was 650, because at the end of the roll call a German said '*650 Stück, alles in Ordnung*' [650 items, everything in order]. I do not remember who carried out the roll call, that is to say whether it was the officer or the soldiers.

I am sure the departure took place on 22 February, not only on the basis of what I wrote in the book I have mentioned, but also on the basis of a letter, of which I retain a copy, that I wrote immediately after my return to Italy to some relatives of mine in America.

I do not remember whether after the arrival of the Germans any contacts took place on our part with the Italian police with the aim of preventing the deportations. During the previous days, we had tried to obtain some guarantees against deportation but only received some extremely vague promises...[1]

After the roll call we were loaded onto buses, together with our luggage, and taken from the camp to Carpi railway station. The SS were with us, our luggage was on the roof of the bus, and on arrival at the station an SS soldier ordered me to climb onto the roof to unload the luggage; at that time I could not make out what the Germans were saying and did not understand the order; the soldier hit me and violently forced me to climb onto the roof.

I think that I was transported from Fossoli to Carpi in one of the first buses. I cannot say whether these buses made only a single journey or a number of journeys between Fossoli and Carpi and vice versa. When I arrived at Carpi station I seem to remember that the train was still almost empty. The Germans had intended that the wagons should be occupied in alphabetical order, beginning with the front one; however, we managed to circumvent this ordering system to some extent, so as not to be separated from some of our friends. I seem to remember that my bus left Fossoli at about 10 in the morning. The train was completely full at about 14.00, but did not leave until about 18.00. Many prisoners who wanted to rejoin friends or relatives in other wagons were brutally beaten.

This order by the Germans to occupy the train in alphabetical order was observed with great strictness, even when

---

[1] (from which it was clear that they had no say in the matter). [Levi's note]

it resulted in the separation of family groups into different wagons. I was kicked and struck with a rifle butt. A colleague of mine who tried to change wagons was slammed against the door-frame of the wagon and wounded in the forehead so severely that he arrived at Auschwitz wounded, with the wound still open.

The train was made up of twelve goods wagons, each of which was occupied by between forty-five and sixty people. My wagon was the smallest and was occupied by forty-five people. An occupant of my wagon was able to read a sign hung on the outside of the wagon itself which bore the inscription 'Auschwitz', but none of us knew the meaning of the word nor where that place was to be found.

Our guards travelled in a special wagon, I cannot remember whether at the front or the back of the train, and I do not remember whether it was a goods wagon or a passenger wagon; this wagon also contained the supplies for the journey.

Our guard was composed of SS, at least in part; in fact, our psychological state during the journey was not such as to permit us to make distinctions. I have been told that in 1945 I testified that at least two of the accompanying personnel were SS from the Fossoli camp; it is possible that my memory was fresher then than it is now, and in any case at that time I tried to reply in the most truthful way possible.

I do not remember whether the SS officer that I had seen at Fossoli was with us during the bus journey or later on the train.

The wagons only had a little straw on the floor and no latrine of any kind and no bucket. In our wagon there were some children, and so we had a few chamber pots which enabled us to rid ourselves of excrement through the small window of the wagon. It was possible to leave the wagon only once a day, sometimes in stations and sometimes in open country. In both cases the prisoners had to attend to their personal needs in public, under the wagons or in their immediate vicinity, and with men and women mixed together. The guards were always present. At night, there was barely enough space to sleep lying on one's side on the floor, all pressed up against each other. The wagons had no heating, and frost congealed inside them. At night it was very cold, by day one suffered a little less because one was able to move.

As far as food was concerned, we had been allowed to provide ourselves with a supply of bread, jam and cheese; and with water; the bread and jam were in sufficient quantities to prevent us from suffering from hunger, but there was a great shortage of water because at Fossoli we had had no containers, so everyone suffered badly from thirst. The guards prohibited us from asking for water from outside and from receiving it through the window.

During the entire journey, we did not receive any hot food; simply, during the daily descent from the wagon, two or three men per wagon would be would be taken by the guards to the provisions wagon to collect the bread and jam for their wagon. Only once, in Vienna, were we allowed to renew the supply of water. In our wagon there was a baby who was still being breast-fed and a little girl of three years old; even for them there was nothing to eat apart from the ration of bread and jam. I have been told that there was at least one death during the journey; I do not remember whether it concerned a man or a woman. I was told this circumstance by a doctor friend of mine who was part of the transport. I should be grateful if my deposition of 2 September 1970 could be amended in this respect.

Our convoy finished its journey on the evening of 26 February; the train stopped in the public station of the city of Auschwitz (not at Birkenau or in the central camp). As soon as we got down from the wagons a very rapid selection took place and three groups were formed. The first group, of which I was a member, was made up of ninety-six or ninety-five men who were fit for work; the second group was made up of twenty-nine women fit for work; all the others were judged to be unfit for work.

At the time, I was only able to estimate the number of women fit for work; however, after being repatriated, I received confirmation from women who survived that the precise number was twenty-nine.

The able-bodied men, of whom I was one, were transported by truck that same night to the Buna-Monowitz camp. The largest group, made up of those unfit for work (all the children, the old people and women with children, the sick and the incapacitated), were loaded into trucks and taken to a destination unknown to us. Only some months later, when, in the Monowitz camp, I began to understand German and to take in what my fellow prisoners were saying, did I realize that those unfit for work had all been killed in the days immediately following arrival; this was confirmed for me by the fact that after my return to Italy none of them were ever seen or heard of again.

I attach to the present deposition a note of mine consisting of a list of 75 names that I was able to reconstruct after my return to Italy. It includes 75 of the 95 or 96 men fit for work who entered the Monowitz camp with me. The names circled are of those who survived until the liberation; the names marked with a 't' are those who took part in the evacuation transport which took place in January 1945 from Auschwitz to Buchenwald and Mauthausen; 's' marks the names of those who died in selections; 'm' the names of those who died from medical causes; and 'l' the name of the single prisoner who died after liberation but before repatriation. I have been able to reconstruct the registration number of a few of my companions: in all cases the first digits of the said number are 174. My own registration number was 174517.

Before my arrival in Auschwitz, I did not know the names of the concentration camps and the details of the exterminations which took place there; however, I did have some concrete information about the operation to exterminate the Jews through the following sources:

(1) articles which appeared in Swiss newspapers, in particular in the 'Gazette de Lausanne', which it was possible to read in Italy during the war;
(2) listening to clandestine allied radio broadcasts, especially Radio London;
(3) a 'white paper' published by the English government on German atrocities in the extermination camps, a pamphlet which reached me clandestinely and which I myself translated from English into Italian;
(4) various conversations with Italian soldiers returned from Russia, Croatia and Greece, who had all witnessed mistreatment, killings and deportation of Jews on the part of the Germans;

(5) conversations which took place between 1942 and 1943
     with Jewish refugees from Croatia and Poland who had
     taken refuge in Italy.

On the basis of all these sources of information, at the time
of our deportation we believed that our fate would consist of
a very harsh prison, of forced labour, of a shortage of food,
etc., but we did not foresee that in the concentration camp
such a methodical operation of mass murder would be taking
place, and on so large a scale.

Read, confirmed and signed.

Primo Levi

21

The Europe of the Lagers

Primo Levi

[1973]

The history of the deportation and of the concentration camps cannot be separated from the history of the Fascist tyrannies in Europe: they show that foundation taken to the extreme, beyond every limit of the moral law that is engraved into the human conscience. If National Socialism had prevailed (and it could have prevailed), the whole of Europe, and perhaps the world, would have been caught up in a single political system in which hatred, intolerance and contempt would have reigned unchallenged.

The doctrine from which the camps sprang up was very simple, and therefore very dangerous: every alien is an enemy, and every enemy must be suppressed; and an alien is anyone who can be seen as different, on account of language, religion, appearance, customs and ideas. The first 'aliens', enemies by definition of the German people, were found in the country itself. Already in 1933, a few months after Field Marshal Hindenburg had entrusted Adolf Hitler with the task of forming

---

Editors' title. Published as the introduction to the pamphlet *Museo Monumento al Deportato politico e razziale nei campi di sterminio nazisti* [Memorial Museum to the political and racial Deportees to the Nazi extermination camps], ed. Lica and Albe Steiner (Centro stampa Comune di Carpi, undated but printed in October 1973).

the new government, there were about 50 concentration camps in Germany. In 1939, the number of camps exceeded 100. The number of victims of that period is estimated to have been 300,000, mostly German communists and social democrats, as well as many Jews; primarily intended and feared as instruments of terror, the concentration camps had not yet become centres of organized mass murder.

The beginning of the Second World War marks a turning point in the history of the camps. With the occupation of Poland, Germany enters into possession (they are Eichmann's words) of the 'biological source of Judaism': two and a half million Jews, besides an unspecified number of civilians, partisans and soldiers captured in 'special actions'. This is an immense army of slaves and predestined victims; the end purpose of the 'Lagers' becomes twofold. They are no longer just instruments of repression but, at one and the same time, sinister mechanisms of organized extermination and centres of forced labour, counted on to aid the Nation's war effort. Each of those originally created camps multiplies: new 'external camps' (*Aussenlager*), large and small, are set up, many of which in their turn become centres of propagation, until the entire territory of the home nation is covered with a monstrous network, along with all the countries which, one after another, are occupied and subjugated.

Thus is born, in the heart of civilized Europe and in the middle of the twentieth century, the most brutal system of slavery that the whole of human history can bring to mind. From Norway and from the Ukraine, from Greece and from Holland, from Italy and from Hungary dozens and dozens of trains leave every day; they are packed with 'human material', innocent and defenceless men, women and children, sealed for days and weeks inside goods wagons, without water and without food.

They are Jews, people of all political and religious beliefs, people seized at random in the course of a search. The trains converge on the camps with which, by this time, Germany and the various occupied countries are covered, but only a fourth or a fifth of the new arrivals pass through the barbed-wire fences and are put to work. The others – that is to say all the children, the old people, the sick, the unfit, and the quota that is surplus to the requirements of German industry – are killed with the same indifference and by the same methods with which noxious pests are eliminated. The situation of the deportees who get through the entrance selection and become prisoners (*Häftlinge*) is far worse than that of beasts of burden.

The work is exhausting; one labours in the cold, under rain and snow, in ice and mud, driven on by punches, kicks and lashes; there are no days of rest. There is no hope of a respite; those who fall ill go to the infirmary, but this is the anteroom to death and everyone knows it. A Lager proverb says: 'An honest prisoner doesn't live more than three months.'

Even brotherhood and solidarity, the final strength and hope of the oppressed, break down in the Lager. The struggle is all against all; your greatest enemy is your neighbour, who has designs on your bread and your shoes, and simply by his presence deprives you of a hand's-breadth of pallet. He is a stranger who shares your afflictions but is remote from you; in his eyes you do not read love, but envy if he is suffering more than you, fear if he is suffering less. The law of the camp has turned him into a wolf; you yourself must struggle not to become a wolf, to remain a man.

For this new horror, it has been necessary to coin a new name: genocide; it means the mass extermination of entire populations. But such a result is not easy to achieve. Solving the problem requires the collaboration of the SS administration – by now a veritable State within the State – with German industry.

Towards the end of 1942, the clients and the technicians have decided on the best way to kill millions of defenceless human beings quickly, economically and in silence. It involves hydrocyanic acid in a form already used for some time to rid ships' holds of rats. In great haste, but discreetly, new installations are constructed for an industry never seen before, the manufacture of death. The facilities and their sinister function are exorcised with vague euphemisms: in the official jargon one speaks of 'special installations', 'special treatment', 'emigration to the eastern territories'.

Auschwitz is the pilot camp, in which the experiments made elsewhere are collected, compared and brought to perfection. In 1943, the central Auschwitz camp is in charge of at least 20 'external camps', but one of these, Birkenau

(Brzezinka in Polish), is destined to become famous. It has fortified subterranean chambers into which 3,000 people can be crowded together: these are the gas chambers, in which death by poison occurs within a few minutes. But since it is not easy to make the corpses disappear, there exists too at Birkenau the means of completing the job, a massive incineration plant, the crematory ovens which will subsequently also be built in other camps.

During the months of April and May 1944, 60,000 human beings a day were killed at Auschwitz.

We are dealing here with the very pit of barbarism, and the hope is that what is documented here will come to be seen and remembered into the most distant future as an unrepeatable aberration. It is the hope of every human being that these images may be perceived as a horrific but solitary fruit of tyranny and hatred, whose roots may be recognized in much of the bloodstained history of humankind, but whose fruit will not bear new seed, either tomorrow or ever again.

Figure 7 *La Stampa*, 9 February 1975, first page (by kind permission of the *La Stampa* Archive, Turin).

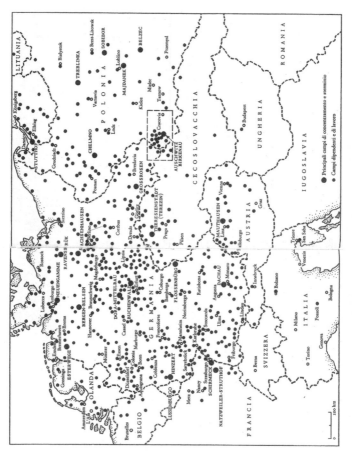

Figure 8 Map of Nazi concentration camps (the borders are those of 1938). Primo Levi published this for the first time in 1973, in the edition for secondary schools of *Se questo è un uomo* [*If This is a Man*].

22

This Was Auschwitz

Primo Levi

[1975]

We have never been many: there were a few hundred of us, out of too many thousands of deportees, when, thirty years ago, we brought back to Italy and displayed to the dumb-struck amazement of our loved ones (those of us who still had them) the pale blue Auschwitz number tattooed on our left arms. So it was true then, what Radio London had reported; it was true to the letter what Aragon had written, 'marqué comme un bétail, et comme un bétail à la boucherie' [branded like livestock, and like livestock to be butchered].

Now we are reduced to a few dozen; perhaps we are too few to be listened to, and besides we often have the impression of being troublesome narrators; sometimes a strangely symbolic dream which haunted our nights of imprisonment even comes true before our eyes: the interlocutor who does not listen, does not understand, becomes distracted, goes away and leaves us alone. And yet we have to tell our story; it is a duty towards our companions who did not return, and it is a task that gives a meaning to our survival. We

Published in *La Stampa*, 9 February 1975. Printed on the front page, it is the newspaper's leading article and is illustrated by a European map of the Nazi Lagers which reproduces the one that Levi included in the schools' edition of *Se questo è un uomo* [*If This is a Man*] which appeared in 1973 (included here as figure 8).

have happened (not through our own merit) to live through an experience of fundamental significance and to learn some things about Man which we feel it is necessary to divulge.

We know that man is an oppressor: he has remained that way despite thousands of years of law codes and courts. Many social systems try to curb this impulse towards iniquity and the abuse of power; others, on the contrary, praise it, legalize it and hold it up as the ultimate political aim. These systems, without any distortion of terms, can be described as Fascist; we know other definitions of Fascism, but it seems to us more accurate, and more in line with our own individual experience, to define as Fascist all and only those regimes which deny, in theory or in practice, the fundamental equality of rights between all human beings; now, since the person or class whose rights are being denied is seldom resigned to it, under a Fascist regime either violence or fraud becomes necessary. Violence, to put down the inevitable opposition; fraud, to confirm to the faithful that the abuse of power is laudable and legitimate, and to persuade the downtrodden (within the ample limits of human credulity) that their sacrifice is not really a sacrifice, or else that it is indispensible for the sake of some vague and transcendent goal.

The various Fascist regimes differ between themselves as to the predominance of fraud or, respectively, of violence. Italian Fascism, its first-born in Europe and in many respects its pioneer, erected, on the initial foundations of a not especially bloodthirsty repression, a colossal edifice of mystification and fraud (anyone who was a student during the Fascist period retains a searing recollection of it), the effects of which remain to this day. National Socialism, profiting from the Italian experience, nourished by distant barbaric ferments and catalysed by the demonic figure of Adolf Hitler, directed itself towards violence right from the start, rediscovering in the concentration camps, old institutions of slavery, an 'instrumentum regni' endowed with the desired potential for terror, and continuing down that road with unbelievable speed and consistency.

The facts are (or should be) well known. The first *Lagers*, hurriedly set up by the SA right from March 1933, three months after the rise of Hitler to the Chancellorship; their 'regularization' and multiplication to a hundred or more on the eve of the war; their monstrous growth, in both number and size, in conjunction with the German invasion of Poland and the western part of the USSR, which contain 'the biological source of Judaism'.

From those months onwards the *Lagers* change their nature: from instruments of terror and political intimidation, they become 'bone-mills', instruments of extermination on a scale of millions (four at Auschwitz alone), and are organized industrially, with installations for mass poisoning and crematory ovens as large as cathedrals (up to 24,000 corpses burnt in a single day at Auschwitz, the capital of the concentrationary empire); then later on, in correlation with the first German military reverses and the consequent shortage of manpower, a second transformation takes place in which, alongside the ultimate (and never repudiated) aim of the extermination of political adversaries, there coexists the aim of creating a gigantic army of unremunerated slaves, forced to labour till they die.

At this point, a map of occupied Europe induces a feeling of vertigo; in Germany alone, there are hundreds of *Lagers* in the strict sense of the word – that is to say those from which normally no one escapes alive – and to these are added the thousands of camps intended for other categories; one only has to think that interned Italian soldiers alone numbered around six hundred thousand. According to Shirer's estimate, there were at least nine million forced labourers in Germany in 1944.

The camps were not, therefore, a marginal phenomenon; German industry depended on them; they were a fundamental institution of Fascist Europe, and the Nazis, for their part, made no secret of the fact that the system would have been maintained, and indeed extended and perfected, if the Axis had won. It would have been the complete realization of Fascism: the consecration of privilege, of inequality and of the negation of liberty.

Even inside the *Lagers*, a typically Fascist system of authority was set up, indeed was deliberately created: a strict hierarchy among the prisoners in which the greatest power was reserved for those who worked the least; every job title, even the most derisory (sweepers, scullions, night watchmen) was conferred from on high, while the subject – that is to say, the prisoner without rank – was completely devoid of rights; and nor was there lacking a sinister offshoot of the secret police in the form of a multitude of informers and spies. In short, the microcosm of the camp faithfully reflected the social fabric of the totalitarian State, where (at least in theory) Order reigns supreme: nowhere was more ordered than the *Lagers*. I certainly do not mean to say that our past makes us detest order in itself, but rather *that* order, because it was order without rights.

With all this behind us, hearing talk today of new orders and black orders is strange for us; it is as if the things that happened had never happened, as if they meant nothing and were useful for nothing. And yet, the atmosphere of the Weimar Republic was not so different from our own; and yet, from the first rudimentary *Lagers* of the SA to the fall of Germany, the breakdown of Europe and the 60 million dead of the Second World War, no more than twelve years went by. Fascism is a cancer that spreads quickly and it threatens to return; is it too much to ask that we should oppose it at the start?

23

Political Deportees

Primo Levi

[1975]

Every large regional subdivision of the Reich had its own annihilation camp: Mauthausen for Austria, Dachau for Bavaria,
Buchenwald for Thuringia, Belsen for Hanover, Flossenbürg
for the Bohemian Forest, and Auschwitz for Silesia. Some
of them – Gross-Rosen, Ravensbrück and Sachsenhausen –
were reserved almost exclusively for women. Each camp had
a main nucleus and a number of subordinate camps (Arbeit
Kommandos) spread throughout the surrounding region.

The registration of the deportees was consecutive for each
camp; transports between the main camp and the various
Kommandos were very frequent, but less frequent between
one camp and another, in which case registration, which in
some camps took place by means of tattooing, would change
as well.

The Hitlerian madness regarded not just a particular
person or group of people but rather an entire race as an

Published in *Torino contro il fascismo. Testimonianze* [Turin against
Fascism: Testimonies] edited by the city council and by the Comi-
tato per le Iniziative Antifasciste della Città di Torino (the City of
Turin Committee for Anti-Fascist Initiatives), printed in Turin on 25
April 1975, the thirtieth anniversary of the Liberation.

Political Deportees, like the previous text, *This Was Auschwitz*,
was accompanied by a map showing the 'Locations of German
Concentration Camps'.

enemy to be fought, and the camps, especially Auschwitz, became the cemetery of the Jews. Added to them very soon were the Spanish anti-Francoists captured by the Germans during the civil war and, from the time of the annexation of their respective countries, the Austrian and Czechoslovakian patriots.

From 1939, Nazism regarded as political enemies the patriots of the various occupied nations who felt duty-bound to resist the invader, and from that point on the German lagers became filled with partisans from the whole of Europe, a veritable international aristocracy of freedom fighters, firstly the Poles, then the French, the Belgians, the Luxembourgers, the Greeks, the Hungarians, the Romanians, the Soviets, the Yugoslavs and finally, after 8 September 1943, the Italians. Being the last to arrive did not alleviate for our fellow countrymen the harshness of their stay in the camps. The percentage of Italians who died was in fact no lower than those of other nationalities, and came to around 93%.

In every main camp, and in the majority of the Arbeit Kommandos, there was a crematory, to which corpses transported from Kommandos not so equipped would also flood in. Despite this, the incineration of the bodies took place at a much slower rate than the deaths, so the corpses piled up in great numbers in the courtyards which divided the various sections, and were then also disposed of in mass graves.

There were about 50,000 deportees from Italy, including the 25,000 Jews (men, women and children) deported to Auschwitz, of whom only about 1,000 came back.

Most of the other deportations from Italy had Mauthausen as their destination, where almost 10,000 patriots met their deaths, with 730 survivors, a great many of whom also passed away after being repatriated as a result of disease and of the hardships they had undergone.

The first batch of fifty deportees was sent to Mauthausen from Turin in December 1943; this was reported in brutally exultant tones by the Repubblichino news-sheet 'Il Popolo di Alessandria' [The People of Alessandria]; there were two survivors.

In February 1944, there were numerous deportations of political detainees and of the resisting workers of Sesto San Giovanni from the San Vittore prison in Milan; in March, a convoy of more than 700 patriots left Turin, largely made up of Fiat workers and of the organizers of the strike which, in the first of those months, paralysed the industries forced to work for the Germans, besides a large group of partisans captured in action in the Val di Lanzo.

After that, the deportations increased at a fearful rate from month to month. For the most part, deportation would take place a few days after arrest, without trial but not without an interrogation according to German methods at the Albergo Nazionale or in Via Asti in Turin, at the Albergo Regina or the Villa Triste in Milan; before crossing the border in sealed wagons, the patriots would undergo a stay of several days in the Fossoli camp near Modena (where in July 1944 as many as sixty-nine patriots were mown down by machine-gun fire, among them the son of the late Senator Gasparotto), or else in Bergamo prison or in the Bolzano camp. This would encourage an influx of blankets, clothing and provisions, which the Germans would advise prisoners to request from their families on account of the privations which awaited them. As soon as they reached the camp, the prisoners would be stripped even of their last garment, searched, their heads shaved, and made to dress in prison uniform; their nationality would be distinguished by an initial inside a red triangle sewn next to their registration number, and this also served to differentiate the political detainees from the common felons who were marked out by a green triangle. The job of surveillance inside the various sections of the camp was reserved for the common felons, who were mostly German and picked from among the most savage criminals, and who would be issued with cudgels and rubber batons if necessary.

The SS were in charge of external surveillance, and twice a day carried out a count of the deportees.

The reveille took place at four in the morning and work began at six, for the most part digging and carrying stones; it would be interrupted for three-quarters of an hour for soup, and would finish at 18.00. The same schedule and the same treatment was undergone by those assigned to work as mechanics, mainly in camps subsidiary to the central ones, where however there would be two twelve-hour labour shifts, of which the night-time one would be particularly exhausting.

After the distribution of bread, which as a general rule took place at about 20 hours, there would be silence; but nightmarish awakenings would take place during the night, sometimes for an immediate departure, but more often for a search of the pallets or a body search, or else simply for the periodic check for parasites. The deportees, completely naked, would then line up in the internal courtyards under the blinding glare of the floodlights, and any real or presumed infractions would be punished by a varying number of baton blows, from five to twenty-five; even the detection of an insect would be punished with the baton, and this was the only method of parasite control practised by our torturers.

The full details of life in the camp can be omitted here, since survivors from every land have written many books on the subject, supported by testimonies and by incontrovertible evidence.

The first camp to be liberated was Auschwitz on the part of the Russian army. The last was Mauthausen, which saw the joint action of American and Russian troops.

The fact of being the last camp to be liberated was fortunate for Mauthausen, since the Germans, as long as they had the chance, tried to evacuate the other camps just as the Soviet or Anglo-American advance was on the point of liberating them. And such evacuations were really and truly mass annihilations! It is enough to say that, when the Soviets were about to liberate Auschwitz, the deportees were made to set off in long lines of moving corpses along the roads of Silesia and Czechoslovakia all the way to Mauthausen, which a few of them (not even a hundred out of many thousands) reached alive on a night of very severe weather and were left standing until dawn in the courtyard of the shower block because, before being taken into the huts assigned to them, hygiene demanded that they bathe.

In relation to this subject, we should also say that Mauthausen experienced extermination by means of the gas chamber mainly in April 1945, when in little more than three days about 10,000 prisoners were gassed. At other times, the gas chamber at Mauthausen was limited in its operation. At Auschwitz, on the contrary, this summary method of liquidation was employed every day, and the numbers are consequently very great: over 5 million gassed in about five years!

When, during the bleakest months of 1944, the state of mental and physical degradation in which the deportees were kept made any hope of salvation seem like madness, when the constant presence of death – in the physical form of the corpses which night after night everyone might find by their side in the pine bunk which was so like a coffin – had by this time stripped away any closeness to life, replacing it with a strange, resigned familiarity with death, now taken for granted as a friend, an admonition arose, detached and solemn: struggle to survive, because it was vital that, on the inevitable day of the triumph of liberty, at least one among so many should still be alive in order to spend the remainder of his powers in a mission which would vindicate the sacrifice of the others by bringing to the world the knowledge and the horror of an ideology which denied equality and parity of rights between human beings, of a system which held in contempt the fundamental demands of Christian civilization, annihilating the dignity of Man and threatening to spread throughout the whole world the enslavement of the extermination camp.

24

Draft of a Text for the Interior of the Italian Block at Auschwitz

Primo Levi

[8 November 1978]

The history of the Deportation and of the extermination camps, the history of this place, cannot be separated from the history of the Fascist tyrannies in Europe: from the original burning of the Italian Camere del Lavoro [Chambers of Labour] in 1921, through the bonfires of books in the public squares of Germany in 1933, to the iniquitous flames of the crematories of Birkenau, runs an unbroken link. It is ancient wisdom, of which Heinrich Heine, a Jew and a German, had already warned us, that those who burn books

---

Text prepared for the Italian Memorial in the Auschwitz Lager: two typed pages, unsigned, dated '8 November 1978' and preserved as a photocopy in the Centro Internazionale di Studi Primo Levi [International Primo Levi Study Centre], Turin.

The Italian Memorial was opened on 13 April 1980. Much shortened and revised, Levi's contribution was carved on a stone, without a signature. Here is the transcription: 'Visitor, / observe the remains of this camp / and take thought: / from whatever country you come, / you are not a stranger. / See to it that your journey / has not been in vain, / that our deaths / have not been in vain. / For you and for your children / may the ashes of Oświęcim / serve as a warning: / make sure that the monstrous fruit of hatred, / of which you have seen the traces here, / may not bear new seed, / either tomorrow or ever again.'

will end by burning human beings; violence is a seed which will not die.

It is sad but necessary to remind both others and ourselves that the first European experiment in the suppression of labour movements and the sabotage of democracy had its origins in Italy. It is Fascism, unleashed by the crisis following the First World War, by the myth of the 'mutilated victory', and nourished by ancient miseries and wrongs; and Fascism will give birth to a growing delirium, the cult of the man of destiny, organized and enforced enthusiasm, the entrusting of every decision to a single will.

But not all Italians were Fascists: we, the Italians who died here, bear witness to that. Alongside Fascism, another unbroken thread had its origins in Italy before anywhere else: anti-Fascism. Bearing witness with us are all those who fought against Fascism and suffered on account of Fascism, the martyred workers of Turin in 1923, the prisoners, the internees, the exiles, and our brothers of all political creeds who died resisting the restoration of Fascism by the National Socialist invader. And other Italians bear witness with us too, those who fell on all the fronts of the Second World War, fighting, against their will and in despair, against an enemy who was no enemy of theirs, and realizing too late that they had been deceived. They too are victims of Fascism: unwitting victims.

We were not unaware. Some of us were partisans and political fighters, captured and deported during the final months of the war, who died here while the Third Reich crumbled, lacerated by the thought that liberation was so near. Most of us were Jews: Jews who came from every Italian town, and also foreign Jews, Polish, Hungarian, Yugoslav, Czech and German, who in Fascist Italy, where anti-Semitism was enforced by Mussolini's racial laws, met with kindness and civilized hospitality from the Italian people. They were rich and poor, men and women, healthy and sick. There were children among us, many of them, and old people on the threshold of death, but all of us were loaded like goods into wagons, and our fate, the fate of whoever passed through the gates of Auschwitz, was the same for all. It had never happened, not even in the darkest of ages, that human beings were exterminated in their millions like noxious insects, that infants and the dying were sent to their deaths. We, the Christian and Jewish children (though we do not care for these distinctions) of a country which had been civilized, and which became civilized once more after the night of Fascism, bear witness to this here.

In this place where we innocents were killed, the very pit of barbarism was plumbed. Visitor, observe the remains of this camp and take thought: from whatever country you come, you are not a stranger. See to it that your journey has not been in vain, that our deaths have not been in vain. For you and for your children may the ashes of Auschwitz serve as a warning: make sure that the monstrous fruit of hatred, of which you have seen the traces here, may not bear new seed, either tomorrow or ever again.

25

A Secret Defence Committee at Auschwitz

Primo Levi

[1979]

Many years ago, when I was a prisoner at Auschwitz, I played a part in an incident which to begin with I did not understand. Around May 1944, a new Kapo had been assigned to our work squad: he was a Polish Jew of about thirty, sullen, taciturn and plainly neurotic. He beat us for no reason; in truth, beating was universal down there – in that Babel of an environment, blows were the easiest way of communicating, the 'language' that everyone understood, even the new arrivals; but that Kapo beat us deliberately, in cold blood, in order to cause pain, with a subtle cruelty meant to bring about suffering and humiliation. I commented on this behaviour to a Yugoslav workmate of mine and he gave me a strange smile and said, 'Yes, but you'll see, he won't last long.' Sure enough, a few days later the beater disappeared; nobody ever heard of him again, he had ceased to exist, indeed everything went on just as if he had never existed. But many incomprehensible things happened in the Lager, the very fabric of the Lager was incomprehensible, and I ended by not thinking any more about the episode.

Published in *Ha Keillah* (Turin), 4, 4 (April 1979). Levi returned to this incident in his final book, *The Drowned and the Saved* (1986), at the beginning of the chapter 'Shame'.

The following December, when the thunder of the Soviet
artillery already sounded near, I happened to meet a friend of
mine, engineer Aldo Levi from Milan, whom I had not seen
for a long time. He was in a hurry, I do not remember why,
and I too was in a hurry. He greeted me and said: 'Perhaps
something may be going to happen soon; if it does happen,
look for me.'

This encounter too later became obscured by the dramatic
events of the liberation of the camp; but, together with the
first one, it came back to me again a long time later on a 'civilian' occasion, and indeed a festive one – namely, a reunion
of ex-deportees in Rome. There was a dinner, and sitting
opposite me was a French survivor; he had been in my camp
but neither he nor I remembered having met each other. We
exchanged the usual jokes about how under present-day circumstances it was so easy to find something to eat while back
then it had been so hard. We had both had a bit to drink and
this made us inclined to confide in each other. H. told me that
at Auschwitz-Monowitz he had been part of a secret defence
committee, that many important events in the internal life
of the Lager depended on what they decided, and that as he
was a member of the French communist party, he had been
assigned by the committee to work as a clerk in the Political
Section, that is to say the division of the Gestapo that dealt
with political matters inside the Lager. I asked him whether
the hurried words that engineer Levi had spoken to me might
suggest that he too was part of this clandestine organization,
and H. replied that yes, that was likely, but for reasons of
secrecy each of them did not know more than a very few of
the other members.

I asked him too for an explanation of the episode of the
Kapo who disappeared, and H. gave a smile that closely
reminded me of that other smile of my Yugoslav workmate.
He replied that yes, in some particularly serious cases, and at
grave risk to themselves, they had been able to cancel a name
from the lists of those selected to be sent to the gas chamber
in Birkenau and to substitute a different name. No, he did
not remember the case of our Kapo, but the thing seemed
probable: on other occasions they had caused a spy or a bread
thief to disappear in this way, or had saved in this way one

of the members of the committee. I knew that the laws of conspiracy were harsh but it had never occurred to me that any name whatever, mine for instance, could have served to preserve a life politically more useful than my own. I asked H. if indeed, among the many dangers that I knew myself to have run, there had also been this unknown danger. H. replied: '*Évidemment*'.

26

That Train to Auschwitz

Primo Levi

[1979]

Dear Rosanna,

Even though I do not (as yet) have the pleasure of knowing you personally, I feel like a friend of yours and close to you for many reasons. You have asked me to let 'Gli Altri' [The Others] have an account of the time when I too, like all the Jews of Nazi-occupied Europe, was defined as 'other', condemned, that is to say, to the condition of an alien, indeed of an enemy. I believe that this condemnation, which amounts to an expulsion from the body of the 'normal', always happens from the outside, that no one, or almost no one, naturally feels or becomes 'other'; for which reason it is always painful. This condemnation was extremely painful for Italian Jews, even though less tragic, to begin with, than elsewhere, precisely because they were not and did not feel themselves to be 'other'; they had blended in with the rest of the country for hundreds or even thousands of years, they had the same customs, language, faults and virtues as other Italians, and

Published in *Gli altri* [The Others] (Genoa), 4, 3 (1979), 2nd trimester. Open letter to Rosanna Benzi, the Genoese founder and director of the magazine. Born in 1946, Rosanna Benzi was struck down by poliomyelitis at the age of 14. From then on she lived imprisoned in an iron lung until her death in 1991.

in particular, when confronted by Fascism, they had behaved like the others, which is to say with a resigned or sceptical acceptance, enthusiastic only for a few. In 1938 – at the time, that is, when the racial laws were enacted in Italy – I was a 19-year-old student; the separation from my non-Jewish contemporaries and friends was painful, but (at least for me) not humiliating. The accusations against all Italian Jews which one read in the newspapers were too grotesque to be believed, and in fact they found scant credence among the public, even among convinced Fascists; the Italian people, in this respect, showed itself to be little inclined to accept the certificate of superiority to the Jews which the racial laws had bestowed on it free of charge. Like many in my position, I reacted more or less consciously to the inane accusations of the propaganda by constructing for myself an awareness, and even a pride in belonging to a minority, which I had not possessed before.

Things abruptly got worse in September 1943 when the north of Italy was occupied by German troops. In towns across Italy, a veritable man-hunt was unleashed: squads of German, and unfortunately also Italian, police searched out the hiding places of Jews who had been unable or unwilling to go into exile, often following up denunciations supplied by hired informers. Out of approximately 35,000 Jews then living in Italy, they found 8,000, and those were precisely the most defenceless and unprepared: the poor, the sick, old people with no one to help them. In this, the Nazi persecution was truly savage beyond comparison: in the absurd totality of the slaughter, which did not stop either at the dying or at children.

I was arrested as a partisan in the Val d'Aosta, but was immediately recognized to be a Jew. They took me first to the Fossoli transit camp, near Modena; from here, at the end of February 1944, to Auschwitz: but this name, so terrible today, was then unknown to everyone. Our train, made up of goods wagons, carried 650 people, 50 to a wagon; the journey lasted 5 days, during which food was distributed but not water. When we arrived at the station, we were made to get out; and in a rapid selection, three groups were formed: the men, and the women respectively, who were fit for work (96 men and 29 women) and all the others, which is to say the old, the sick, the children, and the women with children; these, 525 in number, were sent straight to the gas chambers and the crematories without even being registered in the camp. According to what I found out later in the Lager, this ratio of about one to four was more or less constant for all trains: one Jew to work against four to die. So the slaughter was more important than the economic exploitation.

My personal fate, which I have described in my book *If This is a Man*, is very far from being the typical fate of an Auschwitz prisoner: a typical prisoner would die of exhaustion, or of diseases caused by starvation and vitamin deficiency, in the course of a few weeks or months. One only has to consider that the official food ration was about 1,600 calories a day: that is to say, barely sufficient for a man in a state of complete repose, whereas the prisoners were forced to carry out hard labour in a cold climate and with inadequate and unsuitable clothing. I repeat: every one of us survivors is a favourite of fortune. My own good fortune was of several kinds: throughout a year of imprisonment I never fell ill, but I did fall ill at just the right moment, when the Lager was abandoned by the Germans, who for mysterious reasons omitted or forgot to exterminate the sick who were unable to take part in their flight from the advance of the Red Army. I met a 'free' Italian bricklayer who for many months secretly brought me soup and bread. Lastly, during the final months of 1944, which were the coldest, I managed to get myself recognized as a chemist and was assigned to less exhausting and demanding work in an analytical laboratory.

Out of the 96 men who entered the camp with me, 15 survived; out of the 29 women, eight survived: so there were 23 survivors out of the 650 deportees on our train, that is to say 3.5 per cent. Yet it was a fortunate train. Because it left Italy a little less than a year before the liberation: almost no one survived two or three years of imprisonment. The sum of the total numbers, which I learnt only on my return to Italy, but which tallies and is in close agreement with what I myself lived through and witnessed, comes to around 6 million victims, the figure provided by those Nazi perpetrators themselves who did not succeed in escaping justice. Of these, about three and a half million were killed at Auschwitz.

This is the experience from which I have emerged, and which has marked me profoundly; its symbol is the tattoo which I still have on my arm: my name from when I had no name, the number 174517. It has marked me but it has not taken away my desire to live; on the contrary, it has increased it, because it has given a purpose to my life, that of bearing witness so that nothing of that kind can ever happen again. This is the goal to which my books aspire.

27

In Memory of a Good Man

Primo Levi

[1983]

I should like to contribute to the commemoration of a man who has been close to me for many years, who shared my harshest experiences, who gave help to many and asked for help from few, who once saved my life, and who died quietly a few days ago at the age of eighty-five. He was a doctor; I think he must have had thousands of patients during his half-century of professional practice, all of whom have retained a grateful and affectionate memory of him, as you do of someone who has assisted you to the best of his ability, without arrogance and without intrusion, but entering fully into your problems (and not only your health problems) in order to help you overcome them.

He was not good-looking; he was delightfully ugly, something of which he was cheerfully aware and which he exploited as a comic actor might exploit a mask. He had a big, crooked nose and thick, bushy, blond eyebrows which framed a pair of shining blue eyes, never melancholy, almost childlike. In recent years he became deaf, which did not distress him in the least, but even before that he had a way all of his own of taking part in a conversation. If it interested

Published in *La Stampa*, 21 October 1983. It was written on the death of Leonardo De Benedetti, although neither the article nor the newspaper mentions his name.

him, he would participate with courtesy and common sense, without ever raising his voice (which in any case was weak and tremulous even when he was a young man); if it did not interest him, or ceased to interest him, he would let his thoughts visibly wander, without doing anything to hide it; he would withdraw into his shell like a tortoise, leaf through a book, look at the ceiling or stroll around the room as if he was on his own.

But he was never absent-minded, indeed he was very attentive, when he was with his patients. By contrast, his feats of absent-mindedness when on holiday were legendary, and he would recount them afterwards with pride; indeed, he often boasted about his weaknesses, which were few, and never about his virtues, which were patience, affection and a silent courage. Apparently frail, he possessed a rare strength of mind which showed itself more in endurance than in action and which communicated itself invaluably to those who were close to him.

I do not know much about his life before 1943; from then onwards, it was not a fortunate one. He was Jewish, and to avoid being captured by the Germans he attempted, in the autumn of that year, to cross the border into Switzerland along with a large group of relatives. They all managed to pass the frontier, but the Swiss guards were unyielding, admitting only the elderly and the children along with their parents. All the others were escorted back to the Italian border: in other words, into the hands of the Fascists and the Germans. We met in the Italian transit camp at Fossoli and were deported together, and from then on, we did not part from each other again until our return to Italy in October 1945.

On entering the Lager, his wife, who was as gentle, defence-less and quick to defend others as him, was immediately put to death. He declared that he was a doctor, but he did not know German, so he shared the common fate: labouring in the mud and the snow, pushing wagons, shovelling coal, earth and gravel. It was punishingly hard work for everyone but lethal for him, physically weak, out of condition and no longer young. After a few days on the construction site his shoes injured his feet, which swelled up, and he had to be admitted to the infirmary.

Here there were frequent inspections by the SS doctors; they judged him to be incapable of working and put him on the list for death by gas, but fortunately his professional colleagues, the French or Polish prisoner-doctors of the infirmary, intervened: four times they managed to have his name crossed off. But in the intervals between these death sentences and temporary reprieves, he remained as he was, frail but not broken by the brutal life of the Lager, mildly and calmly aware, a friend to everyone, incapable of rancour, without anguish and without fear.

We were liberated together; together we travelled thousands of kilometres in distant lands, and on that interminable and inexplicable journey too his kindly and indomitable character, his infectious capacity for hope and his zeal as a medical practitioner with no medicines were invaluable not only to us, the very few survivors of Auschwitz, but to a thousand other Italian men and women on the uncertain journey back from exile.

Having finally returned to Turin, he stood out from all the other survivors by his perseverance in keeping alive the network of solidarity among his fellow prisoners, even those far off or in foreign countries. From then on, he lived for almost forty years in a situation that only a man like him would have been able to create around himself: single in registry-office terms but in reality surrounded by a multitude of friends, old and new, all of whom felt indebted to him for something: many for their health, others for a wise piece of advice, others still simply for his presence and for his smile, childlike but never unmindful or sad, which lightened the heart.

28

To Our Generation...

Primo Levi

[1986]

To our generation there has fallen the none too enviable
fate of living through richly historic times. I do not mean to
say that *afterwards* nothing else has happened in the world:
natural disasters and mass tragedies caused by human voli-
tion have happened everywhere, but, despite the omens,
nothing comparable to the Second World War has taken place
in Europe. Each one of us is therefore a witness, whether he
wants to be or not; and it has been right and timely for the
Region of Piedmont to carry out a survey of the memories of
survivors of the deportation, since this last-named event, on
account of its magnitude and the number of its victims, has

Text of a speech delivered by Primo Levi on his penultimate appearance in public, on 22 November 1986. Levi was taking part in the
conference 'Storia vissuta' [Living History], organized by the ANED
(National Association of Political Ex-Deportees), which took place
from 21 to 22 November 1986 in Turin.

Levi presented 'To Our Generation...' as a preamble to a text
written for a combined edition of *If This is a Man* and *The Truce*,
which appeared in the United States as *Survival in Auschwitz and
The Reawakening: Two Memoirs*, published in January 1986 by
Summit Books, New York. *I sommersi e i salvati* [*The Drowned and
the Saved*], to which Levi makes an explicit reference at the end of
his speech, had been published by Einaudi in May 1986.

come to be seen as unique, at least until now, in the history of humanity.

I have been asked to take part in my twofold capacity as witness and writer. I feel honoured, but also weighed down by a sense of responsibility. When you read a book, it may be entertaining or it may not, it may be informative or it may not, it may or may not be remembered or reread. As a writer about the deportation, this is not enough for me. From my very first book, *If This is a Man*, I have wanted my writing, even if I have put my own name to it, to be read as a collective work, a voice which represents other voices. Yet more: that it should be an opening, a bridge between us and our readers, especially if they are young. It is pleasant for us ex-deportees to sit at table together and tell each other about our now long ago adventures, but it is not very useful. Yes, for as long as we live it is our duty to speak, but to the others, to those who were not yet born, so that they can understand 'that it can come to this'.

It is therefore not by chance that a major part of my current work consists of a sort of continuous dialogue with my readers. I get a lot of letters full of the question 'why?'; I am asked to give interviews; above all, and especially by the young, I am asked two fundamental questions. How could the horror of the Lagers have come about? Will it happen again?

I do not believe in the existence of prophets, readers of the future; anyone who has so far claimed to be any such thing has failed miserably, often to a ludicrous extent. Even less do I see myself as a prophet or an authorized interpreter of recent history. None the less, these two questions are so pressing that I have felt duty-bound to attempt an answer, indeed a whole bunch of answers: the ones of which copies have been handed out on the occasion of this conference. Some of them are replies to Italian, American and English readers; others, and they seem to me the most interesting, are the result of an intricate epistolary network of mine which for many years has put me in contact with the German readers of *If This is a Man*. They are the voices of the children and grandchildren of those who committed the deeds, or who allowed them to be committed, or who did not trouble themselves to find out about them. Some are the voices of Germans of a different kind, who did the little or the much that lay in their power to oppose the crime that their country was committing. It has seemed right to me to give space to both the former and the latter.

We survivors are the witnesses, and every witness is required (also by law) to answer in a comprehensive and truthful way; but for us it is also a question of moral duty, given that our ranks, which were always meagre, are becoming diminished. I have tried to carry out this duty with my recent book, *The Drowned and the Saved*, which perhaps some of you have read, and which will soon be translated at least into English and German. This book too, which is made up of questions about the deportations (and not just the Nazi one) and of attempts to find answers, forms part of the colloquy which has engaged me now for more than forty years; I feel it is completely in harmony with this conference. I hope that, in the opinion of its readers, it addresses the real subject of the conference: that is to say, that it brings its modest contribution to an understanding of the history of today, whose violence is the child of that violence which, by sheer chance, we managed to survive.

Appendix: The Train
to Auschwitz

Primo Levi and Leonardo De Benedetti

The following two documents are not only a remarkable feat of memory; they are also the result of a tenacious investigation which Primo Levi began immediately after his return from deportation, looking for his fellow prisoners and getting in touch with them in person or by correspondence, inquiring everywhere for information about the people who had travelled with him to the Lager, or had been confined with him in Buna-Monowitz (the men) and in Birkenau (the women).

The first page comes from Primo Levi's private papers. It is a copy of the list delivered on 3 May 1971, in Turin, to the German prosecutor Dietrich Hölzner who – during the preliminary phase of the Bosshammer trial – had come in person to Italy to question Primo Levi, Leonardo De Benedetti and other Auschwitz survivors. During the interview with the judge, Levi himself explained the nature of the document:

> I attach to the present deposition a note of mine consisting of a list of 75 names that I was able to reconstruct after my return to Italy. It includes 75 of the 95 or 96 men fit for work who entered the Monowitz camp with me. The names circled are of those who survived until the liberation; the names marked with a 't' are those who took part in the evacuation transport which took place in January 1945 from Auschwitz to Buchenwald and Mauthausen; 's' marks the names of those who died in selections; 'm' the names of those who died from medical causes; and 'l' the name of the single prisoner who died after liberation but before repatriation. I have been able to reconstruct the registration number of a few of my companions: in all cases the

first digits of the said number are 147. My own registration number was 174517.

There are actually 76 names on the list. Fifteen years later, in the chapter 'Useless Violence' in *The Drowned and the Saved*, Levi would provide an important detail about his journey: 'The convoy on which I was deported in February 1944 was the first to leave from the Fossoli transit camp (others had left earlier from Rome and Milan, but we had not heard about them)'.[1]

The second document was entrusted to the historian Italo Tibaldi. It is an exact copy of the list prepared for Hölzner, a copy entirely handwritten by Levi with two explanatory notes by De Benedetti at the head and foot of the page. It is preserved in Milan in the Fondazione Memoria della Deportazione [Foundation for the Memory of the Deportation].

[1] Primo Levi, *The Drowned and the Saved*, trans. Raymond Rosenthal (London, Michael Joseph, 1988), p. 87.

L'originale è stato consegnato al giudice Hölzner, poi l'istruttoria - Boßhammer.
3/5/'71

1- Barabas t 174473	26 Halpern	51 Otviste t
2- Bassani B. t	27 Hochberger t	52 Passigli ◊
3- Bassani E. ◊	28 Israel t	53 Ravenna p. ◊
4- Bassani F. ◊	29 Jaffe m	54 Ravenna f
5 Baruch I m	30 Jona 511	55 Revere ◊
6 Baruch II t	31 Lamprenti ◊	56 Rotstein ◊
7 Baruch III t	32 Lenk ◊ 514	57 Sacerdoti t
8 Benjachar ◊	33 Levi A. I ◊	58 Schlesinger t
9 15 m	34 Levi A.II t	59 Schlechoff
10 Campagnano ◊	35 Levi P. 517	60 Segre Tullio ◊
11 Carmi t	36 Levi Sandro ◊	61 Sermoneta t
12 Cittone t	37 Levi Sergio t	62 Simkevic t
13 Coen G. ◊	38 Lewinski	63 Steinlauf ◊
14 Dalla Volta A. t 48	39 Levi Lelio ◊	64 Tedeschi ◊
15 Dalla Volta G. ◊	40 Lascar I ◊	65 Tedesco I t
16 De Benedetti 489	41 Lascar II ◊	66 Tedesco II t
17 Diena m	42 Lonzana ◊	67 Tedesco III t
18 Foa G. ◊	43 Luria m	68 Valabrega I ◊
19 Fitz m	44 Lusena F. t	69 Valabrega II ◊
20 Flesch m	45 Lusena S. t	70 Valabrega F. t
21 Fernari ◊	46 Mandel	71 Treistman t 554
22 Geiringer t	47 Marieni E. t	72 Zelikewic t
23 Gldeksmann t	48 Marieni I.	73 Zelikowski 565
24 Grassini ◊ 500	49 Moscati	74 Kornicof
25 Gruzdar t	50 Ortona ◊	75 Coen G. m
		76 Melli ◊

Su 76: 14 tornati di cui 7 chimici
26 al Trasporto di gennaio (t)
26 in selezione (◊)
8 di malattia (m)

Italiani		57
Polacchi	● x x x ● x	4
Jugoslavi	x x x x x x	6
Tedeschi	x x x x x	5
Austriaci	x x	3
Altri	x x	
		75

Figure 9 Primo Levi. List of fellow deportees who entered Monowitz with Levi, compiled for Bosshammer trial (1971) (Primo Levi's private papers).

Elenco dei Deportati dal Campo di Fossoli
(21.II.44) giunti ad Auschwitz il 25.II.44 e controllati nel
Arbeitslager di Buna-Monowitz

Barabas 174413	Halpern ~~Ovisto~~	Orvieto t
Banani B. (E)	Hochberger t	Passigli)
" E.)	Israel Liko	Ravenna P.)
" F.)	Jaffe m	" E
Baruch I m.	Jona Remo 174511	Revere)
" II	Kornioch m	Rotstein)
Baruch III t	Lampronti)	Sacerdoti F. t.
Benjashau)	Lenk) 174514	Schlesinger t
Calò Sion. t	Levi Aldo I)	Schlochoff
Campagnano)	" " II t	Sepe Tullio)
Carmi Cesare t	Levi P.	Sermoneta t
Cittone t	Levi Sandro)	Simkovic t
Coen Giorgio)	" Sergio t	Steinlauf)
" Giuseppe	Levi Lelio	Tedeschi)
Dalla Volta A. t 174488	Levi Lelio)	Tedesco I t
" G.)	Luzzati I)	" II t
De Benedetti L.	" II)	" III t
Diena m	Lonzana)	Valabrega I)
Foa G.)	Luria m	" II)
Fitz m	Lusena P. t	" Franco t
Flesch m	" S. t	Twistman t 174554
Fornari).	Mandel	Zelikovic t
Geiringer t	Mariani E. t	Zelikowski
Glückmann t	" L	
Grassini l 174500	Moscati	
Sruzdez E. t.	Ortona R.)	

I nomi chiusi in rettangolo appartengono a sopravvissuti –

10

Figure 10 Primo Levi, Leonardo De Benedetti. Copy by Levi of list in figure 9 (1971), with undated notes by De Benedetti (Fondazione Memoria della Deportazione).

Afterword: A Witness
and the Truth

Fabio Levi and Domenico Scarpa

At Kattowitz

Il Mese [The Month], an allied propaganda journal printed in London and distributed in Italy, published the following news item in issue 17, dated 7 May 1945:

A government commission made up of Soviet experts, assisted by Polish, French and Czechoslovakian academics, have completed their inquiry into conditions at the Oswiecim[1] concentration camp. About 3,000 survivors of different nationalities have been questioned and, on the basis both of their statements and of the documents found in the camp, the commission has been able to establish that during the period between 1941 and the start of this year, four million people died at Oswiecim. Among the victims were citizens of the Soviet Union, of Poland, of France, of Belgium, of Holland, of Czechoslovakia, of Yugoslavia, of Hungary, of Italy and of Greece...The report goes on to state that the majority of those deported to the camp were killed immediately, put to death in asphyxiation chambers. An average of one out of six were selected for labour. The camp covered an area of about 300 hectares and was able to hold about 250,000

---

[1] Oświęcim ('Auschwitz' in German) is the name of the Polish town on the outskirts of which the extermination camp arose.

people. The retreating Germans took with them about 60,000 prisoners from the camp; more than 10,000 of those that remained there were liberated by the Russians. Seven hundred kilograms of women's hair were found, ready to be sent to Germany.[2]

This was just after the Liberation. In those same weeks, the facts reported in the article quoted gradually received more and more accurate confirmations from various sources. As to the numbers, these would be verified and to some extent reduced by subsequent investigations, although the shocking significance of the first accounts from Poland would not be negated in any way. Moreover, the article just quoted offers a particular contribution by enabling us to grasp the larger picture within which to place the 'Report on the Sanitary and Medical Organization' of the Monowitz Lager, with which this book begins.

The authors of this text, Leonardo De Benedetti and Primo Levi, experienced similar circumstances which for long periods of time were closely shared. They were both Turinese Jews who were arrested after 8 September 1943 by the Fascist militia, the former after having been turned back at the Swiss border with his wife Jolanda, the latter in the Valle d'Aosta where he was part of one of the first partisan bands to have been formed in that region. Transferred to the transit camp for Jews at Fossoli di Carpi, near Modena, on 22 February 1944, after some weeks of internment, they were loaded onto the same train of deportees, the destination of which was Auschwitz.

The same fate, therefore, but with different histories and ages: De Benedetti, a medical practitioner, was then 46 years old; Levi, a recent graduate in chemistry, was 24. For eleven months, they managed to survive in the Monowitz camp (Auschwitz III), where the Nazis were employing the slaves of the Lager to build a synthetic rubber factory, the Buna, which would never go into production. On the approach of the Russian army in January 1945, both Leonardo and Primo were left to die among the thousands of the sick who lacked

[2] 'Four Million Dead in the Oswiecim Camp', in *Il Mese* [The Month] (London), 3, 17 (May 1945).

the necessary strength to join the evacuation march which the Nazis imposed on all the healthy prisoners in the camp. So, on the arrival of the liberators, they were able to embark on the long journey which – together, and after months of wandering through Europe – would bring them back to Turin.

At Kattowitz, more precisely in the infirmary of Bogucice, Leonardo and Primo worked together: Leonardo as a doctor and Levi as his assistant. They were approached in the spring of 1945 by the 'Russian Command of the concentration camp for Italian ex-prisoners at Kattowitz', who asked them for a report to be sent 'to the government of the USSR', detailing the 'operation of medical services in the Monowitz Camp'.[3] We do not have direct evidence of this document, apart from what we can derive from subsequent versions. We do not even know if it was handed over to the Russians in Italian or if it was translated, presumably into the language best known by both authors – which is to say, French.

The interest which the Soviet command took in the testimony of doctors should be emphasized; in fact they were credited, owing to the nature of the profession which they practised, with having the detachment indispensable for giving a clear and objective account of the facts, especially when it came to analysing the treatment endured by the millions of bodies – souls seemed in this context to be far less important – crowded together by the Nazis in the camp system.

A Scientific Account

So that first report on Auschwitz took the road to Moscow and it would certainly be worthwhile to track it down in the archives in which, perhaps, it is still preserved, along with the many others that accompanied it. However, it also travelled to Italy in the scanty luggage of the two survivors,

[3] The document quoted here is a typewritten copy of the 'Report', without either date or signatures, preserved in Turin in the Archive of the Istituto piemontese per la storia della Resistenza e della società contemporanea 'Giorgio Agosti' ('Giorgio Agosti' Piedmontese Institute for the History of the Resistance and of Contemporary Society).

Levi and De Benedetti, since it reappeared, slightly revised, shortly after their return to Turin, which took place on 19 October 1945.

An early copy of the *Report* was presented, almost certainly at the very beginning of 1946, to the historical section of the Comitato di Liberazione Nazionale [Committee of National Liberation; CLN] which had its headquarters in Turin; it is still preserved in the Archive of the Istituto torinese per la Storia della Resistenza [Turinese Institute for the History of the Resistance]. Its aim is to be analytical and informative. References to the authors as 'we' are not at all numerous and for the most part concern the journey to the Lager. Otherwise the discussion avoids individual cases in order to concentrate on the relationship between conditions in the camp and their pathological effects, deliberately ignoring any other extraneous factor. This gives rise to a horrifying picture of the pathologies most widespread at Monowitz. But it also sharply and coherently impresses on the reader the logic that underpinned the 'hospital' system of the camp. Between a maniacal concern for appearances – a real obsession for the Nazis – and a systematic resort to the elimination of the weakest, everything was organized so that the average survival of deportees should not exceed a few months.

After having cast a light on the suffering imposed on an endless mass of human beings, the 'Report' does not hesitate to describe also the culmination; it tells of the lethal pulsation of the gas chambers and the never-ending smoke of the crematories; it even describes the work entrusted to the members of the Sonderkommando, saying of them that they were 'picked from amongst the worst criminals, convicted of serious and bloody crimes', and conjuring up their 'utterly savage appearance, just like wild animals'. It would take more time for even witnesses as careful as Levi and De Benedetti to be able to correct this mistake, not about the existence of the special squads, nor about their dreadful task, but about their provenance; only much later would they learn that these were Jews like the rest, expressly chosen by the Nazis to empty the crematories.

The logic of the pseudo-medical system set up in a camp such as Monowitz was nothing more than a logic of annihilation, of what you could call controlled annihilation. And the

'Report' does not hesitate to speak of 'the annihilation of the Jews' right from the very first lines, in order that there should be no doubt about the overall implication of the facts. Yet the copy presented to the historical section of the Turinese CLN was catalogued under a heading which ended by diminishing the significance of what it was intended to convey: in fact, on the original folder of the document we find written in pencil, 'Fascist atrocities', as if there was no other way to classify an extreme and still largely unknown event except by including it within an already established category. This was also done – and the problem, let it be quite clear, was not confined to Turin, but was far more widespread in Italy, in France and elsewhere[4] – by those who had fought against Fascism but were unable to grasp either the nature or the scale of the persecution visited on the Jews.

It was in order to counter such ignorance that the plan was hatched to publish that first systematic account of the reality of Auschwitz, or rather of the 'sanitary and medical organization' of the camp, in a medical journal. The choice fell not on a highly specialized publication with few readers, but on *Minerva Medica* which presented itself to the reading public as a 'Weekly Gazette for the Medical Practitioner', and therefore reached a rather wider audience well beyond the confines of Turin. However, it was necessary to go further, and at this point the task did not call simply for a doctor or even a chemist: it demanded the pen of a writer. Primo Levi, who for some time had been considering the idea of relating his own experience as a deportee in its broader human implications, took up the challenge. The proof of this new undertaking is also among the papers of the historical section of the Turinese CLN, and it too is preserved in the Archive of the Turinese Institute for the History of the Resistance. In fact, in the same folder that contains the 'Report', separated by a few other pages, is a typed copy of 'The Story of Ten Days': the final chapter of *If This is a Man*, but the first that

---

[4] See in particular, in this regard, Annette Wieviorka, *Déportation et génocide: entre la mémoire et l'oubli* [Deportation and Genocide: Between Memory and Forgetfulness] (Paris: Plon, 1992), 'Les statuts des déportés' [The Status of the Deportees], pp. 141–58.

Levi felt the urge to write. On the final page of the 'Story', under the handwritten signature of the author, can be read the date: February 1946.[5] Which is to say that the two texts should be considered in parallel: conceived, written and made public during the same period, neither of them can be considered as the preliminary to the other. They are comparable but independent.

The 'Report', begun and brought to completion in collaboration with Leonardo De Benedetti and having shared an eventful journey, was now fulfilling its scientific purpose. 'The Story of Ten Days' was something very different: a literary venture solely by Primo Levi. It does not seem a coincidence that 'The Story of Ten Days' is set in an infirmary – indeed, in that very infirmary at Monowitz. If the 'Report', with its impersonal and generalized tone, described the non-human experience 'of someone who has lived for days during which man was merely a thing in the eyes of man',[6] 'The Story of Ten Days' closes with an account of men who 'in the evening, around the stove' felt themselves 'become men once again'.[7] Two different but complementary ways of explaining Auschwitz to someone who has not been there or who refuses to believe. In Italy, the 'Report' was soon regarded as a primary source of *If This is a Man*, almost a preamble to it, overlooking a little too much its self-contained, autonomous and very specifically targeted character. Correspondences were looked for and found between the contents of the one and the other, particularly in the parts of the 'Report' with the greatest number of autobiographical references. It was noted that the explicit descriptions of the gas chambers and the crematory ovens were not repeated in Levi's major work. Due weight was given to the more scientific and impersonal style of the text written with De Benedetti, which led to the particularly sober tone of the writing; and this very distinction was called

[5] The same date is given in the note on *Se questo è un uomo* [If This is a Man] in Primo Levi, *Opere* [Works], ed. Marco Belpoliti (Turin: Einaudi, 1997), vol. I, p. 1375.
[6] Primo Levi, *If This is a Man*, trans. Stuart Woolf (New York: Orion Press, 1959), p. 205.
[7] Ibid., p. 204.

on to confirm and – one could say – to date to its source Levi's capacity to act as a bridge between the exact sciences and the humanities.

Another question then emerged in the commentary on the 'Report', even if with less insistence because of the difficulty of finding an answer: between Levi and De Benedetti, who had written what? That the doctor had dealt especially with diseases seemed only too obvious. It was a question instead of identifying what could be attributed to the future writer: the more direct references to the authors' experiences, added at the beginning and the end and probably written after the return to Turin? The passages (in truth rather infrequent) marked with some flash of irony or sarcasm? Or could one even hypothesize a complete revision of the text on the part of the future writer, at the risk of doing an injustice to the far from hesitant pen of the doctor?

When people have lived through very similar experiences, identifying themselves in a text by a double signature perhaps means simply this: that they feel jointly responsible for these words. It means that a sort of common matrix is being recognized here; which is undoubtedly what the 'Report' was for both Levi and De Benedetti. A matrix moulded on their shared experience, as well as on that of many others; one with which, however, it was all the easier to identify because of the effort of objectivity that had gone into shaping it. Levi almost certainly took from it a stylistic reflex which would be decisive for his future as a writer-witness: the impulse to search, even when confronted by the most troubling facts, for the universal meaning of things. But one can say the same for De Benedetti, who with the 'Report' had tested out how efficacious an objective approach to disease would turn out to be, even in the toughest of situations; he would always preserve within himself that lesson, destined to make of him – that 'good man',[8] as one day his friend Primo Levi would describe him – an excellent doctor.

---

[8] Primo Levi, 'Ricordo di un uomo buono' [In Memory of a Good Man], in *La Stampa* (Turin), 21 October 1983, and included in this volume.

Writings of Primary Intent

Already, therefore, in the two years 1945–6, the 'Report' on Monowitz marked the start of an effort of documentation to which Primo Levi and Leonardo De Benedetti would also show themselves to be committed in the decades that followed, each in his own way but sharing common aims. In the immediate post-war period, the 'Report' was the first witness account of a technical nature to be offered by Italian ex-prisoners of the Lager. In the same way, the other texts collected in this book and signed by the same two authors were also gradually produced (and not all of them published) as the years went by, in order to pass on the irreducible knowledge of the Lager, a knowledge based on precise facts. As writings of primary intent, devoid for the most part of literary ambitions, their purpose was to inform or to raise questions for interlocutors who differed from time to time. When read again today, they help to uncover an aspect of Levi's work which has not been much considered, and which spans a very wide period stretching from 1945 almost up to his death. In fact, they elucidate in an explicit way choices and ideas which, for the most part, are presented less directly in his better-known accounts of deportation. They are therefore helpful in analysing the way in which Levi worked, in dating the first appearance of new ideas and in following their evolution over the course of time, before, that is, those ideas were developed into their final form in *The Drowned and the Saved*, his last book, which appeared in 1986.

The texts by Levi which we have collected in *Auschwitz Testimonies* include articles, witness statements, conference speeches, lectures and other interventions of an official nature: documents of various kinds – printed, in some cases, even more than once, but scattered among the pages of little-known publications and therefore long forgotten.

The first important new insight which this collection offers us – although in truth it is more of a confirmation – can be read immediately after the 'Report'. It involves an unpublished document discovered in the Archivio Ebraico Terracini [Terracini Jewish Archive] in Turin, in the same folder which contains copies of the 'Report' and 'The Story of Ten

Days'. Its title is 'Record by Dr Primo Levi, Registration No. 174517, Survivor of Monowitz-Buna'; it was drafted at the end of 1945, a few weeks after Levi's return to Italy. Its purpose was to offer to the Jewish Community of the city, affected by the extermination, all the news of his fellow deportees that the survivor had been able to gather together up to that point. Levi, in fact, draws up and annotates a list of thirty people who found themselves caught up in the fatal evacuation march from Auschwitz, of which, when he offered his testimony, he still did not know the disastrous outcome. This document is accompanied by a second: a simple list of eighty-four people, men and women, selected for the gas chamber immediately on arrival in the Lager, or deceased during their imprisonment, or missing without further information, or indeed evacuated on the night between 17 and 18 January 1945. Names, in this case, of people who were not Turinese, or on the contrary of whole families from Turin wiped out in the extermination; names of persons unknown, made available to whoever was trying to discover their fate.

These two lists, which are almost certainly Levi's first act of witness after his return to Turin, are a gesture of pity and restitution which was to be repeated many times in the following decades. This modest sense of human worth flows through every name, every item of information, lined up on those pages with the scrupulous care which was innate in Primo Levi. The mark of his style can be gathered from a tap on the space bar stamped into the ribbon of his typewriter: the one that separates the first name on the list, 'ABENAIM from Tuscany' – a surname and place of origin for anyone who was looking for him – from the words 'he was skilled as a watchmaker'. Not 'watchmaker' or 'he was a watchmaker', but: 'he was skilled'. A recollection which is already the outline of a portrait in the fragment of a line: a quality and a human fact, a concrete apposition, a distinguishing mark in a document of moral identity, a trade practised well and with goodwill. And it is here that Primo Levi the witness already becomes, at the start of the journey which we document in this collection, the Primo Levi who was skilled in more complex trades: who did not limit himself to collecting the facts but questioned them, cross-referenced them, put them into reciprocal relationships, drew from them an increase in humanity as well as an increase in knowledge. This 'Record' adds a new dimension to Levi's work at the same time as it reconfirms it – a man animated by a rare interest in what men are and what they are skilled at doing.

Testimonies for Trials

In the months during which the 'Report' was slowly beginning to circulate, and many of the names which his original Turinese 'Record' had just delivered from oblivion were preparing to migrate into the pages of *If This is a Man* – Alberto, Clausner, the 'Pikolo', the child Emilia Levi, Sergeant Steinlauf, engineer Alfred L. – Primo Levi found the path which would prove to be the most congenial in the course of his life: that of a literary writer. But without therefore renouncing any other opportunity to give an account of his own experience of deportation: in the first place, the trials of Nazi criminals, conducted among a thousand difficulties during the post-war period. Levi was in fact convinced that these trials were the most suitable place to bring to justice those responsible for the atrocities perpetrated by Nazism and Fascism, and he was just as convinced that he ought to offer his own contribution, if possible by taking part in the hearing in person, or at least through written depositions.

Even though he strongly wished to do so, he was not able to be present in Warsaw in '47, when Rudolf Höss, Oberscharführer of Auschwitz, was tried and condemned to death. On the other hand, his friend Leonardo De Benedetti was indeed among those called to testify. Included in this book are the declarations drawn up by both of them prior to the trial, in a sphere of close proximity into which they would be brought again, many years after the Höss trial, when they found themselves together in 1970–1, on the occasion of the judicial inquiry into Friedrich Bosshammer, one of those bearing the greatest responsibility for the deportations from Italy. However, in the meantime they had to some extent followed different routes, with Leonardo, thanks to his direct knowledge of the facts and of the man, having, around '59, contributed to the charges against Josef Mengele, while Primo had in '60 sent his own statement to the court of Jerusalem in the lead-up to the Eichmann trial.

For Levi, in that as in other cases, taking part in court proceedings entailed respecting a strict code. Above all, it was important to offer precise information, which involved a careful selection of the details about which one could feel absolutely sure, at the cost of reducing one's own contribution to a limited nucleus of facts. Then it was preferable to report in detail those incidents in which there was clear and demonstrable individual responsibility, or in which there was certainty about the names of the culprits, or in the event that it might be possible to indicate their physical features: 'I would be able to recognize their faces', one reads, for example, in the 'Statement for the Höss Trial' (1947), regarding the SS men who murdered eighteen prisoners in cold blood before hastily abandoning the Monowitz camp which was about to be liberated by the Russians. Moreover, testimony must demonstrate sufficient detachment, so as to enable the judges, if need be, to make a just distinction between the office held by individual functionaries under indictment and their personal conduct: the 'Statement for the Bosshammer Trial' (1965), for example, emphasizes the constant collaboration offered to the Nazis by the militia of the Italian Social Republic in service in the Fossoli camp; however, in the case of three functionaries, clearly identified by name, it had to be acknowledged that they 'behaved towards us with decency and humanity'.

At this point it will not sound paradoxical that the foremost concern of a witness, on account of the extraordinary delicacy of the task entrusted to him, must be to take account of his own fallibility. Levi was strict with himself – as we will see more clearly later on – so much so that he would weigh up the degree of trustworthiness of his every assertion and rectify systematically any mistakes he might have made on previous occasions.

Major Public Statements

On 3 December 1959, replying in the newspaper *La Stampa* to the letter from a young girl anxious to 'know the truth' about 'German concentration camps', Primo Levi began by exclaiming that this 'is the letter we have been waiting for'; and hastened to offer an emphatic confirmation of what the exhibition about the Lagers – which was just then taking place in Turin – was making plain to the many disconcerted visitors, especially the young ones, passing through the rooms of the Palazzo Carignano. It is striking, however, that on that occasion, despite addressing a seventh-grade schoolgirl whose name does not even appear in the newspaper, Levi declares himself to be speaking in the name of the Associazione Nazionale Ex-Deportati [National Association of Ex-Deportees]; his words have to be understood as an official pronouncement, not simply as a brief reply in a newspaper correspondence. In fact, for him, the letter from the young girl was the sign of an important turning-point. At last a demand for knowledge was being shown, expressed by new potential interlocutors, which was enough to give even those few lines of response the flavour of a major public statement: the sign, slight but unmistakable, that times were changing.

In the article which he wrote a few weeks after his exchange with the young girl, and which at the start of 1960 he entrusted to the *Giornale dei Genitori* [The Parents' Paper], Levi could now assert that 'the voice of truth, far from being lost, is acquiring a new tone and a sharper emphasis'. Without allowing himself a satisfied pause, Levi at once began to consider the best way to present the past to the very young: 'In keeping silent, we have sinned out of laziness and through distrusting the power of the word; and when we have spoken, we have often sinned by adopting and accepting a language which is not our own.'

New arguments presented in a renewed language: from then on this would be Levi's style, whenever it happened that he had the chance to speak. It happened during a short lecture on the extermination of the Jews delivered in Ferrara in 1961 – a lecture destined to find a place in a *History of Italian Anti-Fascism*, where it would be the only contribution dedicated to that theme. It happened again in 1966, on the occasion of the congress of the Association of Ex-Deportees held in Turin, where Levi was given the space to reflect in public – taking on a question then largely overlooked – on the specific nature of the deportation of the Jews as compared with deportation for political reasons.

In the meantime, *If This is a Man* had been translated into other languages, the most important of which was German: *Ist das ein Mensch?* appeared in Germany in the autumn of 1961. In Italy, as in Europe, the possibility presented itself of addressing new interlocutors, willing to listen but not persuaded right from the start, and not part of a circle of friends: young people who were 'blank' pages (one of Levi's favourite adjectives) and who wanted to construct for themselves a believable picture of the world in which they were living.

Thus we arrive at the last three texts of great public importance: the leading article, 'This Was Auschwitz' (*La Stampa*, 9 February 1975), inveighing against the mounting dangers of a drift towards Fascism in the picture of Italian and international politics at that time; the 'Draft of a Text for the Interior of the Italian Block at Auschwitz', written in 1978 and at the centre of the complex political negotiations then taking place around the construction of that Memorial; and finally the speech 'To our Generation...', which, despite its brevity, was of considerable significance, both because it was delivered on what was Levi's penultimate public appearance, on 22 November 1986, and because of the lucidity with which it recalled his 'continuing dialogue' over the course, by then, of forty years and with the most diverse interlocutors.

Questioning His Own Memory

The witness to the Lager is called on to repeat himself. Whether or not put into words, this is the social expectation in his regard on the part of the consumers who call on him to speak or to write: institutions, schools, the media; as for legal tribunals, they implicitly ask him to come out with an identical version of his own story every time. Now, Levi managed never to repeat himself: he never completely fulfilled the expectations of the public; on the contrary, more than once he took it by surprise, setting out multi-faceted and far from comfortable truths – nor did he ever let the attention of others wander. It is also true that, alongside the demand for repetition, the public wants the extra detail, the untold story, and this last was something Levi never failed to satisfy, although always in his own way. Every time he spoke, he managed to say something new, avoiding, however, any recourse to emotive images. His preferred style was a reflective one.

The dialectic between repetition and change also comes up in the texts collected in this book: the fabric remains essentially the same, but countless variations are introduced over the course of time. We will discuss this more fully later on. For now, it is useful to indicate another opportunity offered by Levi's writings: they allow us to learn many things about the roads he travelled down in order to get nearer to the truth.

The first of those roads implies the ability to distance himself from his own experience: 'Primo,' Luciana Nissim Momigliano has said in an interview, 'suffered hunger, cold, blows and fear; he became depersonalized and filled with hatred like everyone else. Only after his return, when he started to write, was he able to detach himself from his own experience and present himself neither as a plaintive victim nor as a vengeful judge.'[9] That self-control was such as to permit a relentless criticism of his own memory, of its mechanisms and its legacy: the memory – as he said in *The Drowned and the Saved* – is a 'marvellous but fallacious instrument',[10] which none the less, if rigorously interrogated, can become a vital source of knowledge of the past, and not only of one's own personal past. But how should we deal with memory, and, first of all, what can it offer us? In this regard, the 'Deposition for the Bosshammer Trial', produced by Levi in 1971, offers us important clues to a method: to his own method.

The text, very detailed because it was the result of a long interview with the public prosecutor of West Berlin, Dietrich Hölzner, seems at first sight to adopt two main registers. In the first place, that of certainties: affirmations put forward with a high degree of certitude which help to build up a coherent account, particularly concerning the stay in the Fossoli camp and the journey to Auschwitz. Then there is the register which we could define as that of uncertainties,

[9] Silvia Giacomoni, 'Primo Levi non era così' [Primo Levi Was Not Like This], interview with Luciana Nissim Momigliano, in *La Repubblica* (Rome), 16 February 1997.
[10] Primo Levi, *The Drowned and the Saved*, trans. Raymond Rosenthal (London: Michael Joseph, 1988), p. 11.

modulated through a variety of expressions intended to pin
down, instance by instance, the degree of approximation of
individual passages in the narrative. We will quote here the
most significant formulations through which these various
cases are defined, each of them playing on a broad scale of
nuances: 'as far as I know'; 'as far as I remember'; 'on about
the 20th'; 'I cannot say precisely'; 'I do not remember the
exact number'; 'I cannot remember whether' (whether the
guards' wagon was at the front or the back of the train);
'we immediately had the impression'; 'I cannot say which of
the Germans'; and others as well. Obviously, the register of
uncertainties too was in the service of the truth – that is to
say, of as truthful a testimony as was possible.

In fact, on closer inspection, the picture is still more
complex than we have been able to demonstrate with these
examples. Every affirmation, certain or less than certain, is
the result of processes of verification – based on memory,
yes, but far from spontaneous or uncomplicated. We can see
some of those processes by the way in which, in this very
deposition, they are signalled in a range of specific cases. How
certain pieces of information were acquired is explained, and
the various sources of information are indicated; and here it is
necessary to say that Levi's already high concern for accuracy
increases every time he has recourse to sources other than
personal experience.

In addition to this, Levi performs two operations which
are as necessary as they are difficult. Firstly, the correction
of errors committed in previous recollections as a witness: 'I
have been told that there was at least one death during the
journey; I do not remember whether it concerned a man or
a woman. I was told this circumstance by a doctor friend of
mine who was part of the transport. I should be grateful if
my deposition of 2 September 1970 could be amended in this
respect.' Secondly, the patient work of recovering information which had been lost: 'I attach to the present deposition
a note of mine consisting of a list of 75 names that I was
able to reconstruct after my return to Italy. It includes 75 of
the 95 or 96 men fit for work who entered the Monowitz
camp with me.' Here the key word is 'reconstruct', a word
which takes us back to the 'Record' drawn up twenty-five
years earlier by 'Dr Primo Levi' for the benefit of the Jewish
Community of Turin.

Comparison with Others: Leonardo

Another way which could be taken to discover new aspects of the truth about the Lager consisted in carrying out determined and methodical comparisons with the viewpoint of others. Information gathered from other sources, properly sifted and verified, could enrich the picture and, by widening the horizon, could encourage a stance more detached from one's own personal situation. It was necessary, however, to know how to cultivate, as far as possible, a broad network of connections; in Levi's case, his marked curiosity about others was probably the lever which allowed him to expand his own knowledge from people to things, and to events which occurred more or less far away from him. All others were not equal, however. There was, for example – as we already know – the 'doctor friend of mine who was part of the transport'. 'We met in the Italian transit camp at Fossoli' – Levi would relate in 'In Memory of a Good Man' – 'and were deported together, and from then on we did not part from each other again until our return to Italy in October 1945.' And a little further on: 'We were liberated together; together we travelled thousands of kilometres in distant lands.' The seal of their friendship seems to be that word 'together', placed there to certify the strength of a relationship destined to transform itself over the course of time. In the Lager, the difference in their ages must have been quite significant, just as it must certainly have had some importance at the time when the already mature doctor and the much younger chemist were writing their 'Report' for the Russians together. Once they had returned to Turin, Primo and Leonardo continued to do many things together: the revision and distribution of the 'Report', the depositions for the trials of Nazi criminals, their first return journey to Auschwitz which they made together in 1965. Not to mention the natural closeness of two men who have been described as being 'like brothers'[11] and who lived

---

[11] Elio Vitale, account given in Milan to Ian Thomson, 15 May 1995: the transcription is in the Wiener Library, London, Ian Thomson Collection, 'Papers re Primo Levi Biography', file 'De Benedetti, Leonardo'.

a few dozen metres away from each other and shared the same group of friends. Even though they did have their differences – for example in their political affiliations or concerning the Israeli invasion of Lebanon, when (it was the summer of 1982) Leonardo showed that he did not share the harsh criticism expressed by Primo against the Israeli government.[12]

On the question of testimony, on the other hand, they were in complete agreement. And despite having elected his friend Primo as a kind of literary spokesman, Leonardo never stopped collaborating with him in reconstructing the events of Auschwitz. It is not for nothing that this book, which opens with their combined signatures, also closes with a text written in collaboration, in which both their hands and their handwriting make themselves physically visible: in the two copies of the already mentioned list – delivered to the German judge Hölzner, who had come to Turin on account of the Bosshammer inquiry – of the male deportees who on the evening of 26 February 1944, immediately after their transport arrived in Auschwitz, were selected for forced labour. Levi had managed to reconstruct seventy-six names out of the ninety-five who were not immediately sent to the gas chambers. On a subsequent copy of that list, Leonardo added in his own handwriting instructions for how it should be read.

In 'In Memory of a Good Man', written by Levi a few days after Leonardo's death, his friend's name does not appear either in the title or in the text. Perhaps, among the many reasons for this choice, one consisted of the difficulty of accepting the departure of someone long felt, at least in a small way, to be a part of himself.

In the Darkest Places of the Lager

And now we come to the third direction in the investigation which Levi never stopped carrying out: the excavation of the

[12] Anna Segre, *Un coraggio silenzioso. Leonardo De Benedetti, medico, sopravvissuto ad Auschwitz* [A Silent Courage: Leonardo De Benedetti, Doctor and Auschwitz Survivor] (Turin: Zamorani, 2008), pp. 51–2.

darkest places of the Lager in order to uncover ugly realities. Realities which he measured out, one step at a time, quickly developing an awareness of just how disturbing and complex were the questions at stake and deciding only after a considerable time – from the end of the seventies onwards – to pause and study them in depth from the point of view both of the facts and of their ethical dimension. In a precursory text, which perhaps for that very reason went unnoticed when it first appeared (it was entitled 'Anniversary' because it was published in 1955, ten years after the Liberation), Levi sadly takes note of the silence which for too long had been stifling the memory of the Lagers: 'in Italy at any rate, the subject of the extermination camps, far from becoming history, is heading towards total oblivion'. That sadness was not slow, however, to turn to explicit, if understated, polemic against the tendency, prevalent at the time, to merge the sacrifice of the fallen during the Resistance with the anonymous end of those deported to the Lagers. 'It is futile' – we read in those two long-neglected pages – 'to call the death of the countless victims of the extermination camps a glorious one. It was not glorious: it was a defenceless and naked, ignominious and filthy death.' But the argument does not stop there: it continues with a stab at the wider implications: 'Nor is slavery honourable; there were those who were able to undergo it unscathed, exceptions to be regarded with respectful wonder, but it is an essentially ignoble condition, the source of almost irresistible debasement and moral shipwreck.'

Aware of the disturbing originality of such an observation, in direct contrast to the idea, so widespread after the war, of good and evil as direct opposites, the author is quick to add a warning: 'But let it be clear that this does not mean lumping together victims and murderers.' And he goes on, once again completely counter to the spirit of the time: 'this does not lessen the guilt of the Fascists and Nazis but, on the contrary, makes it a hundred times worse'. And finally he feels it is his duty to state, exponentially expanding the horizons of the study and of his reflections: 'It is right that these things should be said, because they are true.' So the truth was not only a matter of the numbers and of the most atrocious forms of extermination. There was a truth which was deeper even if less obvious, and it had to be sought out and studied, beyond the filthy acts of the persecutors, also in the conduct, before even in the thoughts, of the victims themselves.

From 1955 to 1961: six long years which brought about developments such as the Eichmann trial, the first event to cause a great stir internationally, or gave rise to comforting symptoms, such as that letter in *La Stampa* from the 12-year-old schoolgirl; but the general attitude towards the subject of the extermination was slow to change. In compensation, Levi's reflections continued, even though almost in solitude, and his arguments became ever more explicit. This time we will read an article published in a more prestigious journal with national prominence, *Il Ponte* [The Bridge]; its title, specifically connected to the events of the day, is 'Testimony for Eichmann'. The text, more extensive and demanding than others – almost an essay – takes up the discussion at the point at which it broke off in 'Anniversary': 'We must not retreat from facing the truth.' Consequently, it is necessary to recognize that: 'As well as being places of torment and death, the Lagers were places of perdition. Never has the human conscience been violated, wounded and distorted as it was in the Lagers.'

Immediately after this, Levi clarifies his reasoning. In the first place, 'many otherwise puzzling details of the concentrationary method begin to make sense. Humiliating, degrading, reducing a man to the level of his entrails' became essential for the Nazis, with the aim of ridiculing the threat represented by their worst enemies, the Jews and the communists: these humiliations would have drawn from a reassured people – from the German people – exclamations such as: 'But these are not human beings, they are puppets, they are animals.'

There was yet more. That definition of the Lager as a 'place of perdition' or – as he put it six years earlier in 'Anniversary' – as a place of 'moral shipwreck' also had to be explained. And here is Levi's reply – it is yet another truth, so shocking that it takes the breath away:

> There was another means of arriving at the same goal of degradation and debasement. The functionaries of the Auschwitz camp, even the highest-ranking ones, were prisoners; many were Jews. One should not suppose that this mitigated the conditions of the camp: on the contrary. It was a selection in reverse: the basest, the most violent, the worst were chosen

and given unlimited power, food, clothing, exemption from work, even exemption from death by gas, provided they collaborated. They did collaborate.

The Reasons for Silence

The relationship between the experience of the Lager and the present-day world forms a fourth axis of reflections which can be traced in the texts in *Auschwitz Testimonies*. From this point of view, the most crushing factor which Levi is often forced to confront is the general silence imposed around the extermination in a world which seems to do all it can to file away that past, as painful as it was unseemly. The word with which the author prefers to denote that absence of attention is precisely that: *silence*, to be understood in the first place as a failure to act on the part of a generation who had been there; who, therefore, at least in part, would have been unable not to know. Silence can also be considered as a more or less conscious behaviour, although in that case it implies specific and ascertainable reasons. Finally, silence returns us to its opposite: words; and if silence is absence, words can make present what they describe, but only if they offer themselves in their most lucid form.

The most painful silence – and again we are quoting from 'Anniversary', 1955 – is the silence

of the civilized world...of culture...our own silence...It is not due simply to weariness, to the attrition of the years, to the normal attitude of 'primum vivere'. It is not due to cowardice. There lives within us a more profound and more worthy impulse which in many circumstances urges us to keep silent about the Lagers, or at least to minimize and censor the images of them, still so vivid in our memory.

It is shame. We are men, we belong to the same human family to which our torturers belonged. Confronted by the enormity of their guilt, we feel that we too are citizens of Sodom and Gomorrah....

We are the children of the Europe where Auschwitz exists; we live in the century in which science was warped and gave birth to the racial laws and the gas chambers.

And here once again is the inevitable question to which the argument leads: 'Who can safely say that he is immune from infection?' A question which connects the past with the present and, at the same time, links the factual research on the nature of that infection with the ethical reflection on the responsibility of every one of us.

At this point silence, too, ends by assuming in Levi's view a moral significance, becoming 'a mistake, almost a crime', because 'The shame and the silence of the innocent can mask the guilty silence of the perpetrators, allowing them to defer and evade the judgement of history.' Remarkable and adult words, these last, but they can be read, not by chance, in the letter of '59 to the young girl who asked to 'know the truth'.

Why Speak?

If keeping silent is a blameworthy act in moral terms, testifying offers instead a chance of release. This too is a recurrent theme, not only in Levi's writings but in his daily practice as a writer and, indeed, as a witness. There comes to mind in that regard a saying of Luciana Nissim Momigliano, arrested and deported together with him, which seems to sum up the thinking of them both: 'I was well aware that the fact of having survived Auschwitz had given me far more duties than rights.'[13]

In the first place, then, the duty to speak. But why speak? Or more precisely, in order to say what? How to depict the Lager to the world that came after? The answers are many, but they all take account of fundamental features of that world turned upside down, so hard to understand and to describe. Let us look at the first of them, put to us by Levi

---

[13] Luciana Nissim Momigliano, 'Una famiglia ebraica tra le due guerre' [A Jewish Family between the Two Wars], (Max Heimann Lecture, 'The Holocaust in Italy', 36th IPA [International Psychoanalytical Association] Congress, Rome, 1989), in *L'ascolto rispettoso. Scritti psicoanalitici* [Respectful Listening: Psychoanalytical Writings], ed. Andreina Robutti (Milan: Cortina, 2001), pp. 3–9: 9. (The words quoted here were the ones that concluded the conference.)

in that 'Anniversary' of 1955 – never too often cited, as well as ahead of its time: 'it is not permissible to keep silent. If we keep silent, who will speak? Certainly not the culprits and their accomplices. If our testimony is missing, in a not-too-distant future the tales of Nazi brutality, due to their very enormity, could be relegated to the realm of legends. So, speak we must.' Only words, and especially from those who experienced in person the reality of the Lagers, can vouch for their having existed, the first and essential condition of any further investigation. The silence must be broken for other reasons too. Between our present and the past from which we have come there is a deep connection which we cannot revoke, a bond which gives weight and present-day relevance to Levi's next answer as to why it is necessary to speak about the Lager: 'There have been events which are too significant, we have observed the symptoms of a disease which is too serious for it to be permissible to keep silent.' A disease which attacked the people of yesterday and was with great sacrifice defeated, but which does not in any way promise to spare those of tomorrow.

The 'significant events' of Auschwitz: immediately after offering us this definition, the 'Testimony for Eichmann' shows us the concrete effects which that evil produced: the labour camps, the reduction of the Jews to 'a race of animals', the gas, the crematories.

> But there was yet more and worse: there was the shameless demonstration of how easily evil prevails. This, mark well, not only in Germany but wherever the Germans set foot; everywhere, they showed that it is child's play to find traitors and turn them into satraps, to corrupt consciences, to create or restore that atmosphere of equivocal consent or of open terror which was needed to translate their plans into action.

Even though it seems to be addressed to a particular person, the text which Levi published in 1961 was not intended to lay further criminal charges; it is in fact a testimony *for* Eichmann, not *against* him. This does not mean that Levi was inclined to grant him extenuation, quite the reverse. The objective was to make apparent the reasons why an Auschwitz witness has to continue to lend his endeavours even in a world in which the Lagers have disappeared and even in a hypothetical world to come, completely at peace: so that no new Eichmanns can arise and find a hearing as they spread 'the contagion of evil'. Only in this sense is Levi's testimony 'for' Eichmann; it is a testimony for History (here with a capital letter), which has to be remembered and passed on; it is a testimony against the moral complicity of an entire people; it is a testimony which is ahead of its time in describing to us the collaboration into which Nazism knew how to warp the deportees themselves, and the apparent gratuity of what would one day be defined as 'useless violence'.

Fifteen years later – in the article 'This Was Auschwitz', 1975 – the argument does not change in substance, but the tone and conclusion are to some extent different. One could say that for Levi the survivors of the Lager are the guardians of a truth, indeed of a secret. Consequently, it falls to them to make it the object of a sort of revelation. Only they, in fact, have been able to experience to the bitter end a crucial dimension of human nature. And here is the secret: 'We know that man is an oppressor: he has remained that way despite thousands of years of law codes and courts.'

A Straight Path

Levi was aware of his own authority, consolidated over the years thanks to the many books he published (all differing from each other but animated by the same moral energy) and to conduct consistent with the image of him offered by his writing. And he counted on that authority now that he felt obliged to oppose a danger which, in the article 'This Was Auschwitz', he judged to be impending: 'Fascism is a cancer that spreads quickly and it threatens to return; is it too much to ask that we should oppose it at the start?'

Levi did not consider it his job to offer a detailed historical reconstruction, which none the less is outlined in his article. At the cost of simplification, he believed that it would be more helpful to emphasize the fundamental value of equality, amply demonstrated by an appeal to the historical events which he himself had lived through. Consequently, he considered it was necessary to stress the universal significance of the lesson of Auschwitz – Fascism, like the Lager, was to be regarded as an offence against all humankind – certainly not because he thought that at that time there was any reason to overshadow the centrality of the Jews in the extermination, but because he had always displayed great sensitivity in that regard; the final word of the title *If This is a Man* is testimony to that.

There exists an overall coherence between the approach of the texts analysed up until now and the premise of an especially demanding document, written in 1978. This is the 'Draft of a Text for the Interior of the Italian Block at Auschwitz', based on a memorial effort which was the subject of ever more heated negotiations between the many parties involved. Even in the extreme brevity of the text, the wise tenet which he wanted to offer to the public – an aphorism of Heine: 'those who burn books will end by burning human beings'[14] – is made to arise from a concise historical reconstruction, effective as a piece of literature even though (or indeed because) it is reduced to a few lines. Events in Italy during the years 1920–45, on which the argument turns, escape from a local perspective to take on a European breadth with the underlining of the twofold primacy of the Peninsula, at the forefront both of Fascism and of anti-Fascism. But what counts the most is that the overall picture sketched in this way succeeds in composing the very disparate list of victims of the deportation into a fairly balanced reconstruction, without neglecting anyone and yet without removing from the Jews the leading role to which history, alas, had destined them.

How to Tell the Truth

We have already cited that letter many times, but without ever quoting in full the signature with which the very young sender wanted to describe herself in 'Mirror of the Times', the column about Piedmontese life in *La Stampa*. This is the

[14] The reference is to lines 243–4 of the early tragedy *Almansor* (1821): 'wo man Bücher / Verbrennt, verbrennt man auch am Ende Menschen' [where they burn books, in the end they will also burn people].

moment to close that gap. Here is what we can read below her letter: 'A Fascist's daughter who wants to know the truth'. In his reply a few days later, Primo Levi showed himself to have been especially struck by the final word, and wished to comment on it in this way: 'There is a hunger for the truth, in spite of everything; therefore, we must not conceal the truth.'

The Lager had become a *question of the truth*, and would be treated as such. Levi did not hesitate to reply, speaking of the exhibition about the extermination to which his inter-locutrix refers: 'No, signorina, there is no way of doubting the truth of those images.' And he hastens to set out the concrete proofs which will help to support his certitude: first of all, 'what is left of those evil places'; then the dozens of 'eye-witnesses' present even in a city like Turin – how reductive such a definition sounds today, as if it was only the eyes which could speak! And besides there was also 'the void...left behind' by the thousands of those 'who ended up lost in those mounds of bones': an absence–presence, in short, no less concrete than all the rest. He concludes by saying that the exhibition in the Palazzo Carignano was there to 'dem-onstrate', as one does with a theorem or with any complex question, the real heart of the problem: in this particular case – and here we encounter another of the countless aspects of the Lager – 'what reserves of ferocity lie in the depths of the human spirit, and what dangers, today as yesterday, threaten our civilization'.

So the reply of the deportee-writer seemed at last to spark off a possible meeting between the 'hunger for the truth' of all those represented by the young girl and, on the other side, the urgency of those who were driven by a moral duty to tell not simply their *own* story, but *that* story. But that left open another question of no small account: how could *that* story be told? Levi had certainly not waited until 1959 – the year of the exhibition and the letter – to respond. As we know, he had already given thought to it brilliantly more than ten years earlier in *If This is a Man*, but it will be useful to draw yet again on the texts collected in this book to make some further discoveries about his work as a thinker and a writer.

Let us begin with 'Deportation and Extermination of the Jews'. We are in 1961. In that year, Levi had been invited to

Bologna, on the occasion of a lecture series on the history of Italian anti-Fascism, in order to contribute, along with others, his own testimony. He took part on 13 March, after the lecture by the keynote speaker of the evening, Enzo Enriques Agnoletti, who talked about *Nazism and the Racial Laws in Italy*. When it comes to testimony, it would be natural to expect an account of what the speaker has lived through, and the witness in question certainly did not disappoint the expectations of his listeners: 'When the racial laws were proclaimed, I was nineteen years old. I was enrolled in the first year of chemistry in Turin.' From that point on, however, Levi chose a far from common way to continue the discussion (and it should be remembered that the autobiographical stories of *The Periodic Table* were still to come).

In 'Deportation and Extermination of the Jews', Levi follows the usual itinerary from the enactment of the racial laws to the liberation of Auschwitz, but he articulates it by broadening and narrowing the narrative field from moment to moment, with exact and concise words and with a compelling rhythm mastered to perfection. Few adverbs, no digressions (the only parenthesis concerns the linguistic communication problems 'which caused the very high mortality rate of the Greeks, the French and the Italians'), adjectives reduced to the minimum: nothing but facts, figures, descriptions, names, terse judgements often expressed through verbs of action and the spare precision of the nouns. Essential clues to the psychology of the Lager: of the victims and of the torturers. Reflections rooted in concrete fact, to help the listener to place the personal experiences of the protagonist in the different contexts he found himself in over time; to make comparisons; to reply to questions of proof. This results in a text only a few pages long – a summary of *If This is a Man*, prefaced by some of the stories, *in nuce*, of the future *Periodic Table* – but endowed with a completeness which enabled it to convey to the audience in Bologna a general overview of the Lager, and impressions and judgements on significant issues, and subjective feelings, and much more besides. Such a proof of his skill as a communicator was to be expected from the author of *If This is a Man*. But what most strikes the reader, even a reader who knows Levi's work inside out, is reaching the final line with the feeling of having read something new.

The Touch of Words

There are many expressive possibilities offered by the skilful use of narrative in an autobiographical mode. But if multiple variations on the same material are the result of careful choices, it cannot but be that the same is true of the repetition even of *that* material. The exemplariness of Levi's voice risks making us forget that such a choice is not to be taken for granted. In his case, the preference for first-person narrative was certainly based on good reasons, consistent with his way of looking at the world and of relating to his interlocutors. Let us look at some of them: direct reference to his own experience certainly enables his readers more easily to understand and to believe in realities which are hard for anyone to accept; placing himself at the centre of a network of relationships with others helped him to describe human beings one by one, and to present not just abstract ideas but the ways in which they are embodied in the behaviour of individuals, and the effects that they produce; reducing to a minimum the distance between Levi the narrator and Levi the protagonist of the narrative also helps to reduce the distance from his readers, who for this reason are especially willing to engage with the author in the close dialogue which he maintained with them.

What should one say at this point about the all-too-widespread commonplace according to which the major part of Levi's texts about the Lager are simply reminiscences? That this is a misleading trivialization. And casting doubt on this label prompts us to ask ourselves another question: whether, that is to say, attaching much too lightly to Levi, the narrator of the Lager, the label of 'witness' does not cause us to undervalue the complex issues – confronted by him, on the other hand, with results which never cease to amaze us – attached to two different pathways which must be carefully distinguished. The first pathway leads to the discovery of the truth, or at least of fragments of the truth, which in his case concerns one of the most impenetrable places in history. The second involves finding a way to shape those truths to make them accessible to an audience which is often reluctant to listen: something in which he can succeed only through the greatest care in expressing himself in his writing, comparable

– Marc Bloch would say – to the finesse of the lute-maker, based on 'the sensitivity of the ear and of the fingers'.[15]

'Who would deny that words, like the hand, have a sense of touch?' the French historian asks on the same page of his *Apologia for History*, one of the most illuminating texts on how to study and recount human events; and he says so by means of an unexpected association which Levi would certainly have been able to appreciate. Just as the lines of the Turinese writer – as we have seen in reading the texts in *Auschwitz Testimonies* and as we have tried to show in these pages – have the critical rigour with which Bloch himself wanted every testimony to be sifted during the research work which precedes the writing, in order that it might finally offer up its gram of truth. So in both these cases, over and above the concern with narrative finesse, we find the centrality of testimony. With an important difference, however: that in bearing witness to the Lager, just such words as 'witness' and 'testimony' risk not holding up, proving to be inadequate because they are too weak. Levi has shown us this in the case of words such as hunger, cold, exhaustion: the use which we make of them in our normal everyday life makes them unsuited to the extreme degree of Auschwitz.

If, then, we want to ask ourselves what is the word most suited to Primo Levi, we will have to go back to the beginning, to the earliest of the texts collected in this book: the 'Report' written for the Russians, the 'Record' drawn up for the Jewish Community of Turin, the depositions made for the Höss trial. In those documents, we rediscover the activity of a man who does not limit himself to recording what he saw – even though with the greatest attention and effectiveness of style – but who, along with his critical work on his own memory, never interrupted for a single moment his research on Auschwitz, questioning people and events on the basis of a method which was no less discriminating for being implicit. It is possible that the pages of *Auschwitz Testimonies* have managed to bring something new to the profile of Primo Levi, a witness and a writer who was also 'skilled' as a historian.

[15] Marc Bloch, *Apologie pour l'histoire: ou, métier d'historien* [Apologia for History or the Historian's Craft] (Paris: Librairie Armand Colin, 1949), p. 4.

Acknowledgements

The editors of this book and the Centro Internazionale di Studi Primo Levi [International Primo Levi Study Centre] first of all warmly thank the heirs of Leonardo De Benedetti and of Primo Levi for their generosity, for the material and information which they have made available to us, and more generally for their constant support at every stage of this undertaking.

We should like to express our gratitude to all the people and institutions that have joined in providing us with material and information, and also carried out research for the benefit of our work, starting with Anna Segre, to whom we owe a significant part of the material by and about Leonardo De Benedetti. Among the heirs of Levi's relatives and friends, we especially thank Manuela Paul, the granddaughter of Anna Foa Yona.

We offer heartfelt thanks to Michele Sarfatti and Laura Brazzo, director and archivist respectively of the Fondazione Centro di Documentazione Ebraica Contemporanea (CDEC) [Centre for Contemporary Jewish Research] in Milan, for research carried out, for their generosity in making material available to us, and for permission to reproduce documents kept in their Foundation; we offer similar thanks to the Fondazione Memoria della Deportazione [Foundation for the Memory of the Deportation] in Milan, to its director Massimo Castoldi and to its archivist Vanessa Matta.

Elisabetta Ruffini, director of the Isituto bergamasco per la storia della Resistenza e dell'età contemporanea (ISREC) [Bergamo Historical Institute of the Resistance and Contemporary Era], carried out dedicated research, providing us with a considerable quantity of archive material. We have also received material and valuable information from Marzia Luppi, director of the Fondazione Fossoli [Fossoli Foundation] in Carpi, and from Franca Ranghino and Silvana Barbalato, the librarian and archivist, respectively, of the Centro Studi Piero Gobetti [Piero Gobetti Study Centre] in Turin.

In Turin, we were always able to rely on the staff of the Istituto piemontese per la storia della Resistenza e della società contemporanea 'Giorgio Agosti' (ISTORETO) [the 'Giorgio Agosti' Piedmontese Institute for the History of the Resistance and of Contemporary Society]: here we would especially like to thank the vice-director Barbara Berruti, the staff of the Andrea D'Arrigo archives, the librarian Cristina Sara, and Tobia Imperato. Among Turinese institutions, our thanks also go to the library of the Department of Anatomy, Pharmacology and Forensic Medicine, Università degli Studi [University of Turin]. Finally, we express our gratitude to Marco Luzzati, president of the Archivio delle Tradizioni e del Costume Ebraici 'Benvenuto e Alessandro Terracini' [Benvenuto and Alessandro Terracini Archive of Jewish Traditions and Customs] for his help in providing us with complete copies of the 'Record' and 'Notes' which Primo Levi drew up in 1945 for the Jewish Community of Turin.

The preparation of this book owes a great deal to the studies and research of Marco Belpoliti and Alberto Cavaglion. We offer special thanks to Martina Mengoni for the texts which she discovered and for the research she carried out in collaboration with our Centre.

Although the editorship of the present volume is under the names of the director and the literary consultant of the Primo Levi Centre, it is the result of the teamwork of all the colleagues at the Centre; in particular, it would not have been possible to get this collection into its final shape without the assistance – technical and scientific – of Daniela Muraca and Cristina Zuccaro.

Fabio Levi thanks Marina Levi; Domenico Scarpa thanks Martina Mengoni for the illuminating exchange of ideas and Marina Mendolia for being an active listener.

The English edition, translated by Judith Woolf, was prepared with the advice of Robert Gordon, in consultation with Fabio Levi and Domenico Scarpa, and was overseen at Polity Press by Paul Young and John Thompson.